Cover: Jack Slade's cabin at his Ravenswood Ranch above Meadow Creek in Madison County, Montana. Captain Jack and his wife, Virginia, had moved from this location to a stone house (nearer Virginia City) prior to his hanging. *Montana Historical Society*

Feuds
on the Western Frontier

Dave Southworth

Wild Horse Publishing

Cover design by Dave Southworth

Library of Congress Cataloging-In-Publication Data

Southworth, Dave
Feuds on the Western Frontier

    Bibliography: p.127
    Index: p.137

1. West (U.S.)—History—Biography.
2. Outlaws—West (U.S.)—Biography.
3. Peace Officers—West (U.S.)—Biography.
4. West (U.S.)—History—Sources.
5. Frontier and Pioneer Life—West (U.S.)—Sources.

ISBN: 978-1-890778-15-6
      1-890778-15-X

Copyright: 2010 by Dave Southworth and Wild Horse Publishing

All rights reserved. Without limiting the rights under copyright reserved above, no part of this book may be reproduced, stored in or introduced into a retrieval system, or transmitted, in any form or by any means (electronically, mechanically, by photocopying, recording or otherwise) without the written permission of the copyright owner.

Contents

PREFACE 1

FEUDS OF THE HORRELL CLAN 3

THE HOODOO WAR 19

THE SUTTON-TAYLOR FEUD 25

REPRISAL IN BELL COUNTY 49

THE LINCOLN COUNTY WAR AND BILLY THE KID 53

JACK SLADE AND THE JULESBURG VENDETTA 75

THE MITCHELL-TRUITT AFFAIR 79

THE PLEASANT VALLEY WAR 83

THE EARP-CLANTON VENDETTA 91

BATTLE FOR THE GRAY COUNTY SEAT 97

THE JAYBIRD-WOODPECKER FEUD 101

BULLETPROOF KILLER AND THE PECOS GRUDGE 109

THE JOHNSON COUNTY INVASION 111

THE DEWEY-BERRY FEUD 117

ACKNOWLEDGEMENTS 125

BIBLIOGRAPHY 127

INDEX 137

WORKS BY DAVE SOUTHWORTH

BOOKS: NON-FICTION

Famous Gunfights of the American West
Feuds on the Western Frontier
Colorado Gold Dust: Short Stories and Profiles
Colorado Mining Camps
Ghost Towns and Mining Camps of the San Juans
Gunfighters of the Old West
Gunfighters of the Old West II
Famous Gunfights of Texas
Leadville

BOOKS: FICTION

Franklin Hall
Rhymes of a Storyteller

VIDEOS

Colorado Mining Camps: A Pictorial Treasure of the
    Gold and Silver Boom
Leadville: The Boom Years
Mining Camps of the San Juans
Cripple Creek and the Mining Camps of Teller County
The Mining Camps of Northwest Colorado
Boulder County Mining Camps: A Look Back
The Mining Camps of Gilpin and Clear Creek Counties
The Mining Camps of South Central Colorado

AUDIO BOOKS

Gunfighters of the Old West
Colorado Gold Dust: Short Stories and Profiles
Billy the Kid and the Lincoln County War
Jesse James and the James-Younger Gang
Doc Holliday and the Earp Brothers

Preface

Basically, a feud can best be defined as a state of bitter, prolonged mutual hostility between two or more families, individuals, clans, tribes or other groups frequently marked by murderous assaults in revenge for some previous insult or injustice. In some cases a quarrel will intensify, as ill will and animosity increase, until both parties engage in battle. Warfare in most feuds is characterized by retaliation for unjust deeds, revenge against the retaliating party, etc., with each faction striving for satisfaction or gratification from its last specific reprisal.

Feuds in the early American West occurred in many forms. There were feuds between families such as Graham vs. Tewksbury. The Lincoln County War was an economic struggle. The communities of Cimarron and Ingalls battled for the right to be county seat. Mitchell vs. Truitt grew from a dispute over land rights. The Hoodoo War (also known as the Mason County War) had ethnic overtones. Two political parties went to war in the Jaybird-Woodpecker Feud. Small cattle ranchers refused to be pushed around by large cattle barons during the invasion of Johnson County. Feuds between individuals were normally settled with less bloodshed simply because there were fewer people involved. Among the myriad of origins are several which are not presented in this book, such as labor wars between unions and business owners, and feuds which arose over disputes in claim rights or railroad rights.

The feuds which unfold throughout the following pages were selected for inclusion based on interest, renown, variety and historical significance. Many of the participants are individuals of much notoriety. The cast of characters includes Billy the Kid, John Wesley Hardin, Jim Masterson, Commodore Perry Owens, Deacon Jim Miller, Wyatt Earp, Pat Garrett, Bill Tilghman and Doc Holliday. Most of the action, however, is created by those of lesser reputations.

At the root of each feud are two or more people, with different opinions, certain that they are right and their opposition wrong. Common sense, litigation and mediators usually did little to resolve unwavering differences. Guns were often the last resort. Actually, they were sometimes the first resort as well. Feuds which have become historically prominent usually have done so because of their gunfights and bloodshed.

Since man first walked on earth, people have congregated in groups. Though groups take many forms, the people who comprise these assemblages are bound together by a certain loyalty. Usually, a family has the strongest bond, but association ties will bind together unrelated people with a common purpose. The common reasoning of a group will think much like an individual does when his life, family, property, honor or pride is endangered. There is nearly always some kind of reaction—either defensive or offensive. A feud can be triggered by a seemingly insignificant incident. Conversely, its origins can sometimes be traced to an episode of serious magnitude. Normally, a feud would germinate (from whatever cause), grow and then blossom to its fullest. Rarely would it simply wilt and die. It usually had to be cut off at the roots by intervention of a third party of greater strength, or by mutual extermination.

"An eye for an eye and a tooth for a tooth" is the oldest code of law enforcement known to man. It was also the code of revenge and retribution across much of the early Western Frontier. To what degree could one consider lawless the act of "taking the law into one's own hands" in places where reasonable legal redress could not be obtained? For example, there were no lawmen, nor was there a judge, in Pleasant Valley when the Grahams and Tewksburys went to war with each other. After considerable mutual extermination, outside law enforcement stepped in to end the feud. To arm one's family or group, or to establish a committee of vigilance for the purpose of self-preservation, does not necessarily constitute a disrespect for the law. The disrespect occurs when the feudists or vigilantes overplay their role as "frontier lawmen." Usually when men take the law into their own hands, they do so until they commit atrocities under the guise of doing what is "lawful." All feuds developed with different scenarios —with both factions believing they had the right to be lawmen, judge and jury.

Feuds have occurred around the world, throughout recorded history. There were many in the early American West. This book presents some of the more significant encounters during the post-Civil War period (from about 1865 until shortly after the turn of the century). The author has attempted to present the workings of frontier justice in these conflicts strictly as historical events without any bias or judgment toward any faction involved. There were always (at least) two sides to every story.

This photograph of early Lampasas, Texas, shows the scene of a gunfight that occurred on June 7, 1877, between the feuding Horrell and Higgins factions. Looking west down Third Street, its intersection with Live Oak Street is at right and the public square at left. Most of the shooting took place at this location and throughout the block of Live Oak Street to the north. *Keystone Square Museum and the Lampasas County Historical Commission.*

FEUDS OF THE HORRELL CLAN

Trouble followed the Arkansas-born, Texas-bred Horrells wherever they went. Much of it was of their own making. "The Horrell War" occurred in Lincoln County, New Mexico, in late 1873 and early 1874. Basically it was a conflict between *Tejanos* (Texans) and Hispanics. "The Horrell-Higgins Feud" which occurred in Lampasas County, Texas, culminated in 1877. Both were bloody affairs.

Between 1839 and 1857 the marriage of Samuel and Elizabeth Horrell produced eight children: William, John, Samuel, Jr., James Martin "Mart", Thomas, Benjamin, Merritt, and Sarah. They were a tough bunch. The Horrell family moved from Caddo Gap, Arkansas, to a ranch near Lampasas, Texas, in about 1857. Eleven years later they packed up their belongings and set out for California with a thousand head of cattle. When they reached Las Cruces, New Mexico, they sold their herd. The oldest son, John (William is believed to have perished during the Civil War), gathered the drovers to pay them their final wages. In a dispute over the amount of his wages, a cowpoke named Early Hubbard killed John Horrell. The family decided to stay in the vicinity, at least for a while. About three months later Sam, Sr., met his demise at the hands of Apaches near the San Agustin Pass in the San Andres Mountains. Soon thereafter the Horrells pulled up stakes and returned to the Lampasas, Texas, area.

John, Mart and Ben married three sisters. Each of the couples had children.

Tom also married but had no offspring. Merritt, the youngest son, remained a bachelor and lived with Mart and his family. The brothers raised cattle in the area along Little Lucy Creek. They were a no-nonsense bunch, and each of the boys was very skillful with firearms. The Horrells were well liked and had many friends.

State Police Chief, F. L. Britton notified Governor Edmund Davis that action was necessary to bring a large gang of rustlers to justice and listed four of the Horrell brothers among sixteen names in his report. Shortly thereafter, two Horrell friends, G. W. and Mark Short were involved in an altercation during which G. W. Short shot the sheriff. When a posse attempted to arrest the Shorts, Ben, Tom and Mart Horrell, accompanied by a number of their cohorts, intervened with guns drawn. The posse had no alternative but to watch in vain as the Shorts rode to safety.

A law enacted in 1871 to "Regulate the Keeping and Bearing of Deadly Weapons" specifically excluded Lampasas County. The Short brothers' incident was the catalyst which prompted Governor Davis to extend the law to include Lampasas County. F. L. Britton sent seven policemen, under the command of Captain Thomas G. Williams, to Lampasas in order to enforce the new provisions.

Bill Bowen, a fugitive from the law, had fled to Lampasas months earlier to seek refuge with his in-laws, the Horrells. On March 14, 1873, Sam, Mart, Tom and Merritt Horrell were having drinks at Jerry Scott's Matador Saloon with several cowboys including Bowen when they were confronted by members of the State Police. Captain Tom Williams and the other policemen had seen Bowen go into the saloon and decided to investigate. After entering the building, they tried to arrest Bowen for wearing a revolver. When Williams approached him and attempted to grab his pistol, gunfire erupted. Captain Williams and Officer T. M. Daniels were killed instantly. The lifeless body of Officer Wesley Cherry crumbled to the ground just outside the door. Another policeman, Andrew Melville, was shot in the street. He staggered into a hotel but would soon die. Three other officers were able to flee. Mart Horrell was injured in the exchange of gunfire. He was taken to his mother's home to recuperate. Within a few days a posse of policemen, headed by Britton, arrived at Elizabeth's home and arrested Mart. They also arrested Allen Whitecraft, Jim Jenkins, Jerry Scott and James Grizell. None of the others could be found. The five prisoners were jailed at Austin. Horrell and Scott were then transferred to Georgetown. Artemisa Horrell was allowed to remain with her husband, Mart, to nurse his wound.

Once Artemisa thought that Mart was capable of riding she notified his brothers. On the 2nd of May a mob of about thirty-five men rode into Georgetown in a show of force. While most of the men were shooting at random in order to

Mart Horrell was wounded in a shootout with police at Jerry Scott's Matador Saloon. *Sarah Harrison Cobb.*

keep townspeople at bay, Bill Bowen smashed in the jailhouse door with a sledgehammer. The prisoners were freed, and the mob rode off into the night. A. S. Fisher, a local attorney, was wounded by a bullet during the jailbreak.

The Horrells decided that it was time to pack up and leave Texas in search of greener pastures. After selling most of their cattle to local businessmen, the clan assembled its wagons and headed west.

In late September of 1873, the Horrells settled along the Ruidoso River, in Lincoln County, New Mexico. They probably could have picked a better spot. There had been several incidents which created friction between Hispanics and Anglos in the vicinity. In the eyes of Ruidoso Valley Hispanics, *Tejanos* (Texans) were as bad as Anglos could be. The feud which unfolded over the next few months was predominately between Texans and Hispanics. It is commonly referred to as "The Horrell War."

The first bloody conflict occurred on the night of December 1, 1873. Sheriff Jacob L. Gylam, a Texan, was called Jack by the Anglos and Jackicito by the

Hispanics. David C. Warner was another Texan who had moved to the valley. They both liked their liquor. So did Tom and Ben Horrell and their buddy Zachariah Crumpton. Having had too much to drink, the group decided to "shoot up" the streets of Lincoln. They were raising quite a ruckus when Constable Juan Martín approached and asked them to surrender their guns. Gylam insulted his fellow law officer and told the group to ignore him. The hell-raisers then headed toward a brothel, shooting their revolvers into the air as they walked down the street. Martín rounded up a mob of fellow Mexicans that included Seferino Trujillo and Juan Patrón. When Martín and his men arrived at the brothel they knocked on two doors of adjoining rooms which were occupied by Tom Horrell and Dave Warner. One or the other shot and killed Martín. Warner was shot to death in the return of fire. When the gunfight started, Ben Horrell and Jack Gylam ran from the brothel. They were chased down the street and cornered by the mob. The Hispanics then riddled both men with much lead. In his report to the Adjutant General, Major John Mason, commandant at Fort Stanton, wrote that "... the Texans were murdered in cold blood, one at least (Ben Horrell, just 20 years old) while on his knees—badly wounded, had surrendered and begged for mercy, was inhumanly murdered by having been pierced by nine balls—his body then taken and thrown across the creek near the town." None of the bodies were removed until the following day. Gylam's body was found with thirteen slugs in it. During the night someone had cut off one of Ben Horrell's fingers in order to steal his gold ring. Prior to daybreak, someone had carved a cross on the forehead of Juan Martín.

Three days later two Mexicans were found dead in a pasture at the Horrell Ranch. The following day, the 5th of December, newly appointed Sheriff Alexander H. "Ham" Mills[1] led a large posse to the Horrell homestead and demanded they surrender. The Horrells refused. Shots were fired by both parties sporadically throughout the day. No one was injured. Ham Mills and his posse returned to Lincoln early that evening, without prisoners.

On the 20th of December, a Saturday night, the Horrells and their friends rode into Lincoln. They went straight to a house where a Mexican wedding dance was in progress. The Anglos poured a barrage of lead into the house, then rode off into the darkness. They left behind four dead and three wounded. Killed were Isidro Patrón (Juan's father), Isidro Padilla, Mario Balazan and José Candelaria.

---

[1] Sheriff Alexander H. "Ham" Mills was appointed without election by Probate Judge L. G. Murphy to fill the term of Jacob L. Gylam. As Mills' wife was Mexican, he was very close to the Hispanic populace of Lincoln.

The wounded were Balazan's nephew and two women, Apolonia García and Pilar Candelaria.

Juan Patrón was educated at the University of Notre Dame, became a school teacher, and was later Speaker of the House in the New Mexico Territorial Legislature. Patrón was involved in both the "Horrell War" and the "Lincoln County War." *Lincoln County Heritage Trust.*

On January 7, 1874, Governor Marsh Giddings posted rewards of $100 each for Zach Crumpton, Jerry Scott and three Horrell brothers (actually there were four). This act "officially" made them fugitives from the law. It also gave anybody the right to bring them in. Six days later L. G. Murphy, J. J. Dolan, William Brady and José Montaño organized a vigilance committee for the purpose of eliminating the Horrells once and for all.

Realizing that their time in New Mexico was limited, the Horrells sold nearly

1,100 head of cattle, a few horses and oxen for the sum of $9,802.50. On the next day (January 20) Sheriff Mills and a large posse of Hispanics surrounded the Horrell ranch. That night, under the cover of darkness, the Horrells slipped away and moved down river to the Casey ranch. One day later, Ben Turner (brother-in-law of the deceased Ben Horrell) and a boy named Edward "Little" Hart made their way to the house of an Hispanic in order to procure some corn. Ben Turner was ambushed and slain.

Realizing that the Horrells had abandoned their ranch, J. J. Dolan and a group of opportunists rode to the site. After pilfering the Horrell house they "confiscated" crops and other items which they hauled back to Lincoln.

Incensed by the course of events, the Horrells decided it was their turn to reciprocate. They sent word to Lincoln that they were heading to town for a "reckoning" with L. G. Murphy, J. J. Dolan, Steve Stanley, Ham Mills, Juan Patrón, Juan Gonzales, Bill Warnick and Joe Haskins. Most of the men in the Horrell clan departed for Lincoln on Friday, January 30th. They were armed to the teeth. At Picacho, C. W. King, Edward "Little" Hart and Tom Kennan detoured to the Haskins' homestead. When Joe opened the door, they shot him dead as his horrified Hispanic wife watched. At some point on the road to Lincoln, the Texans decided to abandon their plan, possibly because they had foolhardedly given their opponents advanced warning of their coming. They chose to raise a little more havoc, then head to Texas. The Horrells decided to raid the ranches of some of their enemies and steal their horses before departing from New Mexico.

With the wagons full of their women and children (escorted by Merritt Horrell and a few other men) safely out of the area on a southerly route, the rest of the men turned east along the Rio Hondo. They pillaged the ranches of Ham Mills and his half-brother Steve Stanley. They stole whatever horses they could gather and rode hard down river toward Missouri Plaza (Missouri Bottom). When they reached the settlement of Roswell, the Horrells raided the ranches of Van C. Smith and Aaron O. Wilburn driving off all of their horses. The band then turned south along the Pecos River. Along the trail, the Horrells encountered the wagons of five Hispanic teamsters who were freighting corn to the South Spring River ranch of John Chisum. The Horrell bunch assassinated all five Mexicans.

The next target of the Horrell gang was the ranch of Hugh Beckwith at Seven Rivers. Beckwith, like Ham Mills and Steve Stanley, was married to an Hispanic woman. A few miles north of the ranch, the group encountered Robert Beckwith (Hugh's oldest son) from whom they stole a horse, saddle and gun. Shortly thereafter, they ripped down a corral fence and drove off Hugh Beckwith's horses.

Meanwhile, Aaron Wilburn and Van C. Smith had rounded up a posse which began tracking the horse thieves to the south. Wilburn and Smith were both known to be excellent marksmen. Van C. Smith was a former sheriff of Yavapai County, Arizona, and later would become a deputy sheriff under John Behan at Tombstone, Arizona. They recruited additional riders at Seven Rivers. Eventually the Horrells' trail turned west toward El Paso. Realizing that the Horrells would probably sell the stolen stock in El Paso or Mexico, the posse hastened its pace.

At some point, the horse thieves joined up with Merritt Horrell and the wagons carrying the women and children. This slowed their movement toward El Paso. Smith, Wilburn and the posse spotted the Horrell clan at a place called Hueco Tanks, about 30 miles east of El Paso. Once they were within shooting distance, the posse rained lead on the Horrell band. Zach Crumpton was killed instantly. Three other members of the clan were wounded. Fearing for the safety of the women and children, the Horrells waved a white flag in order to negotiate with the posse. Smith and Wilburn agreed that if the Horrells would return their horses, their caravan could proceed without further harm. Smith and Wilburn cut out their horses, then headed north. At this point, it seems as though the Horrell band turned back to the east in the direction of Fort Davis.

Further down the road, the Horrells encountered a tribe of Apaches. The clan drew their wagons together as a defensive precaution. The party of Indians remained at a distance and only observed. While this was happening one of the wounded men died (a fellow named Steele or Still). The Horrells buried him, then built a fire over his grave so the Apaches wouldn't discover it. Eventually the Indians moved on without incident. After they did, the Horrells also left.

The clan headed back to Lampasas County. "The Horrell War" in New Mexico was over, but problems between Anglos and Hispanics would continue. Later (for the murders which occurred at the Mexican wedding dance), the Grand Jury would hand down indictments against Sam and Merritt Horrell, Jerry Scott, Zach Crumpton (who was deceased), Robert Honeycutt, James Wilson, Edward Hart, C. W. King, Thomas Bowen (Bill Bowen), Captain James Randlett, Robert Casey and others. An attempt was made to prosecute Randlett and Casey. Randlett obtained a change of venue to Socorro County, where his case was thrown out of court. Charges were eventually dropped against Casey, and warrants were never served on any of the others.

The Horrell party arrived in Lampasas County determined to keep the peace. Almost immediately, however, there was an altercation with the sheriff and his posse. Merritt Horrell and Jerry Scott were wounded during the conflict about which the newspaper later reported that "no shots were fired by the Horrell party."

Merritt Horrell and Bill Bowen agreed to stand trial for the death of Captain Tom Williams and the other members of the State Police. When the case was finally heard in October of 1876, both men were acquitted. The Horrells were making an effort to lead a peaceful life, for a change. Their passiveness would not last for long, however.

John Pinckney Higgins was a cattleman who earned a reputation as being a tough, unyielding individual. *Center for American History, University of Texas at Austin (W. P. Webb Papers).*

Although the feud between the Horrells and Higgins actually began in 1877, its roots go back four years earlier. The Higgins family first established a ranch in Lampasas County in 1857, about the same time the Horrells did. They were neighbors, and originally they were friends. Several incidents turned the friendship into a bloody feud. John Pinckney Higgins, usually known as "Pink", was incensed in 1873 when the Horrells killed one of his in-laws, the aforementioned State Police Captain Tom Williams. While riding line one day, Pink Higgins heard a distant shot. He decided to ride out and investigate. He found Zeke Terrell butchering a cow with a Higgins brand. Pink Higgins unsheathed his rifle and killed Terrell on the spot. According to legend, Higgins stuffed Terrell's body inside the disembowelled cow, then notified authorities where they could find the occurrence of a miracle, a cow giving birth to a man. Zeke Terrell had been a Horrell employee. Ike Lantier was a former Quantrill raider who cowpoked for the Horrells. While watering his horse one day, he was startled by an approaching rider and drew his revolver. Pink Higgins, who had already drawn his weapon, fired a slug into Lantier's midsection and killed him instantly. On more than one occasion, Higgins accused the Horrells of tampering with his cattle. Tom Horrell was riding through the brush one day when he met Higgins, his henchman Bill Wren and brother-in-law Bob Mitchell. Quick tempered Pink Higgins cursed Horrell and threatened to kill him. According to the story told, the cool-headed Tom Horrell eased back in his saddle and said something like, "Well, three against one wouldn't be much credit to you." Higgins and his cohorts turned and rode off without further confrontation.

January 22, 1877, was a cold day. Merritt Horrell was standing in front of a fire in the back of Jerry Scott's saloon, and was unaware that Pink Higgins had entered the building. Higgins shot Horrell twice, and after he crumpled to the floor Higgins shot him two more times. Merritt Horrell was dead. He never had a

Tom Horrell, a man of calm demeanor, and his wife, Mattie Ann, a proud but boastful woman. *Sarah Harrison Cobb.*

chance to draw or return fire. On the following day a posse of Texas Rangers brought four of Higgins' men into Lampasas for questioning, but Pink Higgins could not be found.

While en route to the Lampasas courthouse on the morning of March 26, 1877, Tom and Mart Horrell were ambushed about five miles outside of town by Higgins men. Tom was knocked from his saddle as a slug ripped into his hip. Mart received a superficial neck wound but was able to valiantly drive off the attackers. Mart helped Tom reach the Tinnins homestead, nearby, then hastened into town to report the incident.

About a month later, Pink Higgins and Bob Mitchell decided that they had been dodging the law long enough and surrendered to authorities. Both were allowed to post bond and return home.

There was another bloody occurrence about the first of June. At daybreak one morning, two of Higgins' cowboys stepped out of a line shack where they

Pink Higgins and some of his men. Back row (l to r), Powell Woods, Unknown, Buck Allen and A.T. Mitchell. Front row (l to r), Felix Castello, Jess Standard, Bob Mitchell and Pink Higgins. *Center for American History, University of Texas at Austin (W.P. Webb Papers).*

had bunked for the night. As they did so, they were shot down by a barrage of rifle fire. One of the men was killed instantly, while the other would live three more days. It is believed that Tom and Mart Horrell and Bill Bowen were responsible for the incident.

Another confrontation took place at the intersection of Third Street and Live Oak Street in Lampasas on the morning of June 7, 1877. Frank Mitchell and his father, Mack, were loading flour at the store of Yates and Brown on Third Street at about 10:00 a.m. Several members of the Horrell bunch had congregated near the well at Public Square adjacent to Live Oak Street. The group included Tom, Mart and Sam Horrell, Jim "Buck" Waldrup and Bob McBee. John Dixon and Rufus Overstreet of the Horrell faction were nearby at the home of Dixon's mother. When Pink Higgins, Bob Mitchell, Bill Wren and Ben Terry rode south on Live Oak Street they were spotted by the men at Public Square. The Higgins men also saw the Horrells. Shooting started immediately as everybody scattered for shelter.

Bill Wren took a slug in one hip but managed to drag himself up a flight of stairs to a second-story window from where he had a better vantage point. Pink Higgins spurred his mount and rode away to recruit help. Frank Mitchell, who was Bob's younger brother, opened fire on the Horrells from the front door of Yates and Brown. One of his shots dropped Buck Waldrup (who would die the following day). Mart Horrell returned the fire and killed Frank Mitchell where he stood.

Sporadic shooting continued for over an hour. At approximately 11:30 a.m. Pink Higgins returned with reinforcements. The men of both factions fortified themselves and nothing much happened after that. Early in the afternoon, impartial citizens were able to talk both parties into a cease fire.

The following month, fourteen Higgins riders raided the Horrell ranch. The Higgins men took positions surrounding the ranch house and bunkhouse from where they poured rifle fire at the Horrells. The Horrell brothers and their men fought back with a vengeance. After a two-day siege, the Higgins' ammunition began to run low. They departed leaving two Horrell men with minor wounds.

On the 25th of July, Carson Graham departed from the Higgins ranch and headed toward Lampasas to purchase supplies. He was ambushed on the road. Beside his body the Horrell brand had been etched into the dirt.

Major John B. Jones, who was commander of the Texas Rangers' Frontier Battalion, rode into Lampasas County with a detachment of reinforcements for the already present Rangers. Jones was determined to end the feud between the Horrells and Higgins one way or another. He exercised the first part of his plan by arresting five members of the Horrell faction. They were kept under guard at the Ranger camp in order to protect them from the Higgins bunch. Jones then arrested Higgins, Mitchell and Wren and put them under heavy guard at a separate location. This method would allow Major Jones to negotiate with each party without them having to come face to face with each other. His plan was successful. Both parties signed letters of truce. The first letter was dated July 30, 1877, and was signed by the Horrell brothers:

> Lampasas Texas
> July 30th 1877

Messrs Pink Higgins Robert Mitchell and William Wren.
Gentlemen:—

From this standpoint, looking back over the past with its terrible experiences both to ourselves and to you, and to the suffering which has been entailed upon both of our families and our friends by the quarrel in which we have been involved with its repeated fatal consequences, and looking to a termination of the same, and a peaceful, honorable and happy adjustment of our difficulties which shall leave both ourselves and you, all our self respect and sense of unimpaired honor, we have determined to take the initiatory in a move for reconciliation. Therefore we present this paper in which we hold ourselves in honor bound to lay down our arms and to end the strife in which we have been engaged against you and exert our utmost efforts to entirely eradicate all enmity from the minds of our friends who have taken sides with us in the feud herinbefore alluded to.

And we promise furthermore to abstain from insulting or injuring you and your friends, to bury the bitter past forever, and join with you as good citizens in undoing the evil which has resulted from our quarrel, and to leave nothing undone which we can effect to bring about a complete consummation of the purpose to which we have herein committed ourselves.
PROVIDED:—

That you shall on your part take upon yourselves a similar obligation as respects our friends and us, and shall address a paper to us with your signatures thereon, such a paper as this which we freely offer you. Hoping that this may bring about the happy result which it aims at we remain

> Yours Respectfully,
> Thos. L. Horrell

S. W. Horrell
C. M. Horrell

Witness
Jno. B. Jones
Maj. Frontier Battalion

Major Jones delivered the Horrell letter to Higgins, Mitchell and Wren. They responded with their letter of August 2, 1877:

Lampasas Texas
Aug 2nd 1877

Messrs Mart. Tom and Sam Horrell
Gentlemen

Your favor dated the 30th of July was handed to us by Maj. Jones. We have carefully noted its contents and approve most sincerely the spirit of the communication. It would be difficult for us to express in words the mental disturbance to ourselves which the said quarrel with its fatal consequences, alluded to in your letter occasioned. And now with passions cooled we look back with you sorrowfully to the past, and promise with you to commence at once and instantly the task of repairing the injuries resulting from the difficulty as far as our power extends to do. Certainly we will make every effort to restore good feeling with those who armed themselves in our quarrel, and on our part we lay down our weapons with the honest purpose to regard the feud which has existed between you and us as a by gone thing to be remembered only to bewail. Furthermore as you say we will abstain from offering insult or injury to you or yours and will seek to bring all of our friends to a complete conformity with the agreement herein expressed by us.

As we hope for future peace and happiness for ourselves and for those who look to us for guidance and protection and as we desire to take position as good law abiding citizens and preservers of peace and order we subscribe ourselves

Respectfully & c
J.P. Higgins
R.A. Mitchell
W.R. Wren

Witness
Jno B. Jones
Maj. Frontier Battalion

Both factions were ready for peace. Each was sick and tired of the death, destruction, fear and mental anguish associated with the feud. Rarely is a truce between feudists adhered to, but this one was.

Pink Higgins remained in Lampasas until the turn of the century when he moved his ranching operation to the vicinity of Spur, Texas. He was responsible for a couple of other killings (which had nothing to do with the Horrells) before he died of a heart attack at age 66.

Tom and Mart Horrell were arrested for the May 28, 1878, murder of storekeeper J. F. Vaughan, thirty miles west of Waco. The two brothers were locked up in the jailhouse at Meridian on the 8th of September to await trial. On the night of December 15th, a large mob of masked men rode to the jailhouse, whisked past the jailer and with a volley of gunfire assassinated Tom and Mart Horrell in their cells. Many people thought that the Horrells were innocent of Vaughan's murder, but the brothers never had a chance to prove it in court.

Sam was the only remaining Horrell brother. In 1880 he moved back to New Mexico where he raised his six children. Sam Horrell died in California on August 8, 1936.

Major John B. Jones successfully negotiated a truce between the hostile factions in the Horrell-Higgins Feud. Jones, who was commander of the Texas Rangers' Frontier Battalion, also helped establish peace in the Hoodoo War at Mason. *Texas State Library & Archives Commission.*

The community of Mason, as it looked in 1876. *Mason Historical Commission.*

THE HOODOO WAR

Fort Mason, Texas, was officially established on July 6, 1851. It was one of many forts located on the Texas frontier to protect settlers from Indians. The site, on the bank of Comanche Creek about eight miles north of the Llano River was set just above the community of Mason which was named county seat when Mason County was established in 1858.[1] Many German immigrants settled in the area. For the most part, they established ranches and raised cattle. They constructed solid stone buildings for permanence and protection.

Results of the 1860 census showed that Mason County had a population of 630. When votes were cast on February 23, 1861, on the issue of secession, only two votes were recorded "for" while seventy-five were cast "against." Few German settlers were slave owners, and they wanted no part of the slavery issue. When Texas seceded from the Union to join the Confederacy, the Germans in Mason County were generally despised by the non-German element as traitors. As anti-German prejudice grew, two factions emerged—the German and the Anglo. The lines between the factions were quite fuzzy. Though most Germans seemed sympathetic to the Union cause, many fought for the Confederacy. The Civil War years marked a period of many Indian atrocities in Mason County. White settlers, both German and Anglo, banded together to protect themselves from the Indians. Nevertheless, animosity between Anglos and Germans was real.

While most of the ranchers and cowboys from Mason County were off

---

[1] For a short while prior to the Civil War, General Robert E. Lee was commandant at Fort Mason.

fighting for the Confederate Army, their cattle would drift away by the thousands. Some people made a living out of rounding up strays and selling them at market. Later, when laws were passed requiring all cattle brands to be recorded, some of these same people became cattle rustlers. After the ranchers and cowboys returned from the battlefields, there became some assemblance of control over their herds. When the massive cattle drives began, they crossed the vast open range of Mason County on their way to the cowtowns of Kansas. Local ranchers faced the new difficulty of preventing their cattle from joining the herds that passed through. Ranchers faced another problem during cold winters. Severe weather would often cause cattle to drift south. As they crossed the open ranges other cattle would join them. Sometimes these herds numbered in the thousands.

By 1872 Mason County ranchers had begun to string miles and miles of barbed wire fencing in an effort to control their herds. These wire fences heightened the discord which already existed between ethnic groups. Furthermore, it pitted cattleman against cattleman. In some cases, the barbed wire prevented access to water. When wire crossed the path of a herd being driven to market, cowboys would normally cut the wire rather than change direction. An increasing number of cattle rustlers in Mason County added to the amount of fence cutting, as well as the number of flared tempers.

Mason County had been divided, neighbor against neighbor, cattleman against rustler, German against Anglo, and even brother against brother. The stage was set for much violence in what was to be called the Mason County War, more popularly known as the Hoodoo War.

In late 1875, a local rancher, Tim Williamson, was arrested for rustling by Deputy Sheriff John Worley. While Worley, a lawman of German descent, was escorting Williamson to jail they encountered a large and angry mob. Williamson never had a chance to prove his innocence, nor did he ever reach the jailhouse. Without making any attempt to break up the mob, Worley stood by and watched as they shot Williamson down in cold blood. The execution raised the ire of Williamson's friends.

One such friend was Scott Cooley, who owed a lot to the Williamson family, possibly even his life. While in Kansas, at the terminus of a cattle drive, Tim Williamson met and befriended Cooley. Williamson offered Cooley employment as a hired hand in Mason County. Cooley accepted, then accompanied the cowhands on their trip back to Texas. While working for Williamson, Cooley became seriously ill with typhoid fever. Mrs. Williamson spent many long days nursing Cooley until his health was restored. He was indebted to the Williamson family. After leaving Williamson's employment, he joined the Texas Rangers where he was a member of Captain R. C. (Rufe) Perry's Company D. Cooley had left the Rangers and was working near Menardville when he received word of Williamson's assassination. Scott Cooley packed up some supplies and rode toward Mason County heavily armed.

Cooley had several friends in the little town of Mason. He spent a few days asking questions and gathering information. Having learned what he wanted, he

A former member of the Texas Rangers, Scott Cooley, was a major participant in the Hoodoo War. *Mason Historical Commission.*

set out for Deputy Sheriff John Worley's place. As Cooley approached the house he spotted two men working on a windless at the well. Cooley who did not know Worley, asked one man his name. His reply was, "Worley." It was the only identification needed. Cooley drew and shot the deputy sheriff to death. Worley's helper plunged into the well. Cooley dismounted and scalped his victim. Uncertain who the next victim might be, fear ran high through the German faction. Other friends of Tim Williamson decided to ride with Scott Cooley. He was joined by

Mose and John Beard, George Gladden and John Ringgold.

Another incident occurred in Mason where mob justice prevailed. Sheriff John Clark had locked up five rustlers who had been caught while driving a herd of cattle that belonged to others. With battering rams, the mob shattered the jailhouse door, then dragged the rustlers into the street. They marched their prisoners about a half mile down the Fredericksburg road. By the time Sheriff Clark and a few others reached the scene, the mob had scattered. Clark found a fellow named Wiggins lying on the ground dead. He had been shot through the head. Three of the rustlers were hanging from a tree limb. Two brothers named Baccus were dead. Clark cut down the third man, Turley, who was still alive. During the commotion of the lynching, the fifth rustler, Johnson, had managed to jump a fence and disappear across a plowed field.

Dan Hoerster was a prominent member of the community and a leader of the German faction. He had become a target of Scott Cooley. One day as Hoerster, Peter Jordan and a fellow named Pluenneke were riding past the Southern Hotel in Mason, a shotgun blast knocked Hoerster out of his saddle. He would die of buckshot wounds from the gun of John Beard. As Beard, Cooley and George Gladden galloped out of town, a slug from the rifle of Peter Jordan shattered Gladden's hand and the rifle he was holding.

Several days later, Sheriff Clark was inside Keller's store on the Llano River about twelve miles south of Mason. Keller, and Clark spotted two men approaching the store. They were recognized as Mose Beard and George Gladden, two of Cooley's men. After Beard and Gladden dismounted, Clark and Keller opened fire from the front door. Gladden and Beard returned the fire, but with nowhere to hide they were hit by many slugs. Somehow they managed to mount one horse and ride away. Clark, Keller and another man trailed the wounded duo. Beard and Gladden were bleeding badly and had to stop. Clark and the others found them shortly. Minutes later Mose Beard died. Gladden had nine slugs in his body, and was expected to die. He was taken by wagon to his home in Loyal Valley. Gladden would eventually recover.

After regaining his strength, George Gladden shot and killed Peter Border, known as a gunman for the German faction. Gladden was captured and sentenced to 99 years imprisonment. Before long, however, he would be pardoned and released.

John Ringgold was arrested and jailed in Burnet County. Evidently, there was no evidence linking him to any of the crimes, and he was released.

Major John B. Jones was commander of the Frontier Battalion, Texas

Rangers, which was comprised of six companies that patrolled approximately four hundred miles of border. When the governor asked the Texas Rangers to intervene and shut down the trouble in Mason County, Major Jones was selected for the task. With a detachment of forty men (ten from Company D and thirty from Company A) Jones rode to Mason. Jones launched a massive manhunt for Scott Cooley. After two weeks of searching, and no trace of Cooley, Jones realized that his men were not taking the search seriously. Most of the detachment was in sympathy with Cooley, who had ridden with Company D when he was a Texas Ranger. Reluctantly, Jones called his men together to make them an offer. He advised them that any man who was in sympathy with Scott Cooley and who did not wish to pursue him could step forward and receive an honorable discharge. About fifteen men took Jones up on his offer.

John Clark, having had his fill of violence, resigned from the office of sheriff and left Mason County. John Beard also fled the area. Some say he went to Arizona. Through the mere presence of Major Jones and the Texas Rangers, the Hoodoo War came to an end. Scott Cooley disappeared. Some say he became ill and died the following year (1876) in Blanco. Others say he lived to a ripe old age in New Mexico.

Creed Taylor, shown above, and his sons Hays and Phillip (nicknamed Doboy) were prominent figures during the early years of the Sutton-Taylor Feud. *The Center for American History, University of Texas at Austin.*

THE SUTTON-TAYLOR FEUD

Following the surrender by General Robert E. Lee at Appomatox in 1865, thousands of dejected Confederate soldiers turned toward home. The beaten and downtrodden warriors hadn't received a paycheck in ages, their clothes were torn and ragged and their feelings ran high with animosity. Their ill will was not only targeted at the Yankees who defeated them, but often at fellow Southerners who remained at home making money in cattle, cotton and slaves while they impoverished themselves in the army of the Confederacy. When the South failed to fit the mold expected by Congress, they passed the Reconstruction Acts which heightened the agony that already existed in the South. Animosity continued to run high as Federal troops supported carpetbaggers, scalawags and former slaves who were thrown into various governmental positions. In Texas, there was very little social order even after the arrival of the occupation forces. Many former Rebel soldiers set out to re-establish what they felt was rightfully theirs, and some did so with minimal regard for the law and governmental authority.

Prior to the days of barbed wire, Texas cattle roamed free on unfenced open range. Cattle often drifted far from their home range, especially during that time when most of the cowboys were away fighting the war between the states. When a maverick (an unbranded calf) had been weaned, it was fair game for the cowboy who "found" it and applied his brand. The stealing of cattle became big business. Sometimes when cattle were found with brands that were unfamiliar in the area, the finder might register the brand locally and claim ownership of the cattle. Another practice was to register the brand in a different locale, then drive the herd to market at that location. Many rustlers altered brands to make them look completely different. Counterbranding was another means of identification used by the cattle thief. He would cancel the original brand by burning an "x" or diagonal bar through it, and would then apply his own brand as if he had legally purchased the animal. Many former soldiers found rustling to be an easy means to obtain wealth.

Rustlers ran rampant while federal, state and county law enforcement officials did little to stop them. Either they were incapable of doing so or it was a matter out of their "domain." Ranchers decided to take matters into their own hands. Committees of vigilance, called Regulators, appeared in several counties. These forces were often large, heavily armed and occasionally even had the blessing of the governor. Rustlers were not the only target of the Regulators. Their "duties" often included dispensing of known outlaws and others who had been branded as "undesirables." At the top of their "most wanted" list were the sons of Creed Taylor, Hays and Phillip who was known by his nickname "Doboy." The boys were tough, cool-headed and excellent marksmen.

The Taylor boys were continuously in trouble. One incident occurred in an Indianola saloon while Hays Taylor was standing at the bar. A group of black soldiers entered and stepped up to the bar. When Hays advised them that he was not in the habit of drinking with blacks, shooting broke out. Hays shot two of the soldiers then quickly fled the scene. Shortly thereafter, a few miles outside of Indianola, Hays Taylor encountered another squad of black soldiers. They were convinced that he was fleeing from something and wanted him to return to Indianola with them. Taylor refused. A sergeant fired a shot which wounded Hays in one arm. Hays quickly responded by shooting the sergeant who toppled dead from his mule. As the other soldiers scattered, Taylor fled. On another occasion, in November of 1867, Hays Taylor was reading a newspaper while sitting propped against a hitching post, just outside a Mason saloon. Doboy Taylor and several friends were inside partying. As a group of Fort Mason soldiers approached the saloon, one of the privates badgered Hays. The private popped up the brim of Hays' hat and asked him what a damned reb could find of interest in a newspaper. Hays straightened his hat and continued to read. Spurred on by Hays' passive attitude, the private grabbed the hat again and yanked it down over Taylor's eyes. Hays drew and fired as he leaped to his feet. His slug dropped the private where he stood. He was dead. As this happened, one of the Taylor bunch, possibly Ran Spencer, was emerging from the saloon. He also fired, killing a Union sergeant. Major Thompson, the commandant at Fort Mason, arrived at that moment with his pistol in hand. He ordered the boys to surrender. With his usual quickness, Hays Taylor shot Major Thompson between the eyes. One version of this story indicates that the sergeant was actually killed after the slaying of Major Thompson. Regardless, the Taylor bunch rode out of Mason leaving three dead Union soldiers behind.

Buck Taylor (whose given name was William Riley Taylor, Jr.) was a first cousin of Hays and Doboy. His father, William, was one of Creed's brothers. Buck was attending a dance one evening at the home of Joe Tumlinson, his uncle. A squad of Union soldiers approached the house unnoticed. As they stepped through the doorway, a black sergeant pointed his finger at Buck Taylor. Buck drew his revolver and fired, killing the sergeant instantly. Amid the confusion which followed, Buck Taylor escaped to safety through a back door. Buck Taylor was another hunted man who rode with Hays, Doboy and the others.

A substantial reward was offered for the capture of the Taylors. Two fellows named Littleton and Stannard set out to find the Taylors and claim the reward. Littleton had exclaimed, "I will do it or die." Shortly thereafter, Littleton and Stannard were found dead on a road east of San Antonio.

The leaders of two groups of Regulators were summoned to Austin in early June of 1869 to meet with the governor. Jack Helm was a rather unscrupulous individual who led a group of Regulators which had been organized by his boss, A. H. "Shanghai" Pierce, a cattle baron who operated in the area southwest of Victoria. The other leader summoned by the governor was Captain C. S. Bell, a former Union spy and army scout. Helm, Bell and their Regulators, backed by state and Union officials, unleashed a reign of terror across DeWitt County and points south. In Galveston, the *News* reported on September 23, 1869, that "...during the months of July and August they killed 21 persons and turned 10 others over to the civil authorities."

The Choates (who lived in San Patricio County) were friends of the Taylor clan, and were suspected by Jack Helm of harboring some of the Taylor gang. On August 3, 1869, the Regulators attacked the Choate homestead killing John Choate and Crockett Choate and wounding two others. One of the wounded men, F. O. Skidmore, survived after receiving seventeen wounds, possibly the result of a shotgun blast.

After creating plenty of havoc in San Patricio County Jack Helm met C. S. Bell near Yorktown in DeWitt County where the two planned their attack on the Creed Taylor ranch which was located on the Ecleto in Karnes County. Helm and Bell were aware that Hays and Doboy Taylor were in the vicinity but that the fugitives had been camping away from the ranch each night in order to avoid capture. The Regulators put their plan into action. C. S. Bell and his men rode directly to the Taylor place while Helm and the others remained in Yorktown as a diversion. Helm's bunch would follow, in order to arrive at Creed Taylor's house sometime after dawn. It was late Saturday night when Bell surprised Creed Taylor and the women. After placing Creed and the women under guard inside their home, the Regulators hid their horses and then waited in anticipation that Hays and Doboy would arrive in the morning. They were correct in their assumption. At daybreak on the 23rd of August, Doboy and Henry Westfall approached the house on horseback. Hays and their other companions were a short distance behind them. When she heard the horses, Doboy's wife let out a bloodcurdling scream in order to warn them. Doboy and Henry spurred their mounts and raced away amid a hail of gunfire. Hays spotted Creed who had emerged from the house. Believing that his father was in danger, Hays charged the whole posse of Regulators with his gun blazing. One of his slugs hit a posse member in the head wounding him seriously before a barrage of lead took Hay's life. As Jack Helm and the other Regulators rode toward the Taylor place that Sunday morning, they received word that C. S. Bell and his group had departed in pursuit of Doboy Taylor. Doboy and his comrades were able to elude C. S. Bell.

Two weeks later, Doboy and his friends were surprised by another posse at Pennington, Texas. After one of their men was shot to death, Doboy and a fellow named Cook surrendered to the posse. Along the trail to Crockett, Taylor and Cook made a break for freedom, and successfully escaped under the cover of darkness.

Meanwhile, Creed Taylor had been taken into custody by a couple of C. S. Bell's men. Creed was escorted to Helena where he was jailed. After spending approximately one month behind bars, Taylor was released under a bond of $10,000.

The activities of Helm and Bell created such a furor in southern Texas that

Jack Helm felt compelled to publicly justify his actions. He did so in a report which was published on September 23, 1869, in the *Victoria Advocate*:

> "TO THE PEOPLE OF TEXAS: As there has been so much said by the people of the State regarding my operations, and as many know not of what they speak—attributing to me motives that are false—I take this occasion of enlightening the law-abiding citizens as to what I have done, and why I did it. About the first of June I was duly summoned by the military authorities, through Captain C.S. Bell, special officer, to assist in arresting desperadoes in Texas known as the 'Taylor party.' We found this party near the *rancho* of Mr. Creed Taylor and attempted to arrest them. We succeeded in wounding one, Spencer by name, the other effecting an escape. I now proceeded in company with Bell to the City of Austin, where I received emphatic orders to arrest the party. On my return home I found that about forty had collected, in open defiance of the law, determined to resist the legal authorities of the State. I immediately proceeded to summon good citizens to assist me in the capture. The sheriff of DeWitt County accompanied me, myself being deputy sheriff. Both our lives had been threatened by these desperadoes, as well as the lives of all those co-operating with me for their arrest. Mr. Jacobs, the sheriff of Goliad County, had just been killed by members of this same party. Finding that I was ready and determined in action, they divided, separating in squads of from five to fifteen. I proceeded in pursuit of the strongest of these bands, commanded by Jim Bell, a noted desperado of DeWitt County. I succeeded in capturing him and more, who were afterward killed in attempting to escape from the authorities.
>
> "About this time the Peaces—the murderers of Jacobs—were arrested, but subsequently effected an escape. One Stapp was killed in attempting to do so. The Peaces proceeded to the *rancho* of John Choate, in San Patricio County, stating to Choate that they were pursued by a 'vigilance committee', and that they came to him for protection. John Choate now went to the *rancho* of Joe Tumlinson in DeWitt County, fifty or seventy-five miles from his home, and informed Captain Tumlinson that he had left the Peace boys at his house, and that he had loaned them one hundred and fifty dollars with which to effect an escape to Galveston. Choate insisted that Tumlinson should join him; said he had a band well fortified at his house, fully able to whip Jack Helm anywhere. Choate also averred that Helm was a d—d rascal, and had joined the Yankees for popularity, and that he could not raise over thirty men, and they only Dutch and Yankees.

Tumlinson told Choate that he knew Helm to be a good man, acting under proper authority, and that he intended to co-operate with him; that he knew the Peaces to be murderers and thieves; that he had hunted them, and would do so again. Becoming convinced that Joe Tumlinson was not his man, Choate proceeded to the *rancho* of Creed Taylor, about fifty miles distant, where he remained about three days, when he came to the neighborhood of Yorktown, in company with four or five desperadoes, Hays Taylor among the number. Choate now sent word to Tumlinson if he did not join him he would be killed, and that the Yankees had offered twelve hundred dollars reward for him, for the supposed killing of Stapp. Tumlinson replied that if he had done anything wrong he was willing to surrender to the proper authorities of his country, but would have nothing to do with Choate or any of his gang. Choate replied that Tumlinson must risk the consequences of his folly. Choate now went by the house of Jim Bell, and took the clothing and other effects of the Peace boys to his house in San Patricio County. Here he met the Peaces, Fulcrod, the Broolans, Doughtys, Gormans, Perrys, and about forty-two others, all known desperadoes, and many having indictments against them for thieving. Choate informed them that Jack Helm would be upon them, and that they must prepare for a fight. The house was fortified and put in condition for a regular siege, having loop-holes cut on all sides, and secret passages connecting them room to room. They had one keg of powder, five hundred shot-gun cartridges, two hundred Spencer rifle cartridges, preparations for receiving five hundred gallons of water, provisions, and all that was necessary for conducting a siege fifty days by fifty men. I had with me one hundred and twenty-five of the best citizens of the country. Arriving at Choate's a little after day, expecting to have to fight one hundred desperadoes, I immediately proceeded to carry the house by storm. I had one man killed and two wounded in the attack. Crockett and John Choate were killed, and two others wounded. Choate perfidiously attempted to shoot me after he had surrendered, and was killed by myself in defense of my life. I now made all the necessary preparation for interring the dead, which was done. And right here let me nail to the counter those lies that allege that my men disturbed any of Mrs. Choate's property or the property of anyone else. They did no such thing. I encamped in the neighborhood of San Patricio, and conferred with Captain Smith at Corpus Christi. I now proceeded to Yorktown, and sent a report to Helena. I was met at Yorktown by C.S. Bell, and disbanded my force until I could find out the whereabouts of the Taylors. Spent three days in this matter;

collected my men, about twenty-five, and proceeded to the forks of the San Antonio and Guadalupe rivers, where I succeeded in arresting the Hogans, who were members of the same party. I now sent the prisoners to Helena under charge of Tom Flemming and six others. I then proceeded in pursuit of the Taylors. At Yorktown I met Bell, and detailed fifteen men to accompany him, stating to the boys that Captain Bell was a good and true man, and would lead them. I remained in camp with the remainder of my men, to attract attention while Bell could operate. The next morning I took up the line of march for Creed Taylor's, followed by one hundred men. I proceeded by a circuitous route up the Sandies, arresting all persons that I suspicioned, and cutting off all means of escape. I arrived within seven miles of the house, when I received intelligence of the fight with the Taylors. I here disbanded my men, after complimenting them for their orderly conduct, gentlemanly bearing, and devotion to the laws of the country. Taking ten men, I proceeded to Helena, where I met Majors Crosland and Callahan, Lieutenant Thompson, and other gentlemen, who approved of all I had done.

"I and my men are ready at all times to act with the legal authorities of my country in the enforcement of law and suppression of crime. I am a citizen of DeWitt County—deputy sheriff—and am opposed to mob law; but I am ready to give my assistance to the authorities, either civil or military, to arrest thieves and desperadoes who defy the laws, either in Texas or any other part of the United States, regardless of all threats, knowing that the law-abiding citizen is my friend, and the desperado my enemy, which is the only guaranty that I desire to know that I am right. *Jack Helm.*"

In sharp contrast to the report of Jack Helm, F. O. Skidmore wrote (several years later) a very different version of the raid in San Patricio County (which is duplicated here without notation of spelling, punctuation, capitalization or other grammatical errors):

"I was at Choate's ranche, in San Patricio County, Texas, on the 3d of August, 1869. Being an intimate friend of the family, I always stopped there when passing, and convenient to do so, and that was the case on this occasion. Not anticipating any trouble, I went, the 2d of August, 1869, to his house to remain all night; when I arrived at the house Mr. Choate was not at home, but soon arrived, and told me to put out my horse and stay with him all night.

"We conversed much that night about the reports in circulation regarding the high-handed measures of Jack Helm's party. Choate informed me that he had sent off the 'Peace boys,' so that he would not get into trouble on their account; he also said that he would fight any mob, but that any authorized officer—Federal or State—could come and take him and all his effects. I can't say that I saw anything more than usual going on at the house. There were only two men on the place except negroes; there were myself and two small boys, one my brother, aged fourteen years, the other about the same age.

"Helm's party charged the house about daybreak. I awoke at the first sound, and heard them yelling 'Charge!' Immediately several of their number rushed into the house.

"Crockett Choate shot a man named Kykendall. They retired to shelter in out-houses, behind trees and the yard fence. Mrs. Choate then appeared on the piazza, and held a parley with Helm. She informed him that Mr. Choate would surrender if he, Helm, had the authority to make the arrest.

"Helm replied that he was authorized by the highest authority in the State of Texas—orders from military headquarters. Mrs. Choate then informed him that there were three boys in the house who had stopped for the night, and that they were innocent, and for God's sake not to kill them. Helm replied, 'Tell the boys to come out, and they shall not be molested.'

"When I heard that, I went out on the piazza, and spoke to those who confronted me, and I told them that I would surrender, and without a word of warning they commenced firing on me.

"I was shot seventeen times. When I returned to consciousness I was out in the yard near a tree. I crawled to it and sat up against it, and while in this position I was shot at several times; and as I sat there, I saw John Choate receive his first wound. As stated before, Helm said he had authority for his arrest; Choate came out in obedience to this demand, his wife accompanying him, and a little in advance. He raised both his hands above his head, and said, 'I surrender myself and house to the United States authority.' Choate, with the assistance of his wife, retreated to his room. The first wound was in the knee. I saw him no more alive. I was informed that they killed him outright immediately afterwards.

"When Crockett heard Mr. Choate surrender, he broke from the house with his six-shooter in his hand. He ran right past me, all the crowd following him. I then crawled away, and made my escape to a Mexican ranche about half a mile distant from Choate's house.

"About ten o'clock they pursued me there, and carried me back to the Choate house.

"When I arrived there Crockett and the old man were both laid out, dead. I begged them to take me to Mr. Terry's, but they would not. Said they wanted to watch the place. The conducted themselves in an extremely rough and boisterous manner while at the house, appropriating whatever they desired, as if they had killed a robber chieftain and had a right to appropriate his effects. They left me nothing, not even my clothing and pocket change. They stole my saddle, six-shooter, and other things of less note. I cannot say what was taken from the house. Helm talked in a braggadocio style to Dr. Downs, my attending physician.

"The house fronts south; old man Choate was in the east room; Crockett, myself, and the two boys were in the west end. Crockett fired a great many times. John Choate did not fire a gun that I could see or hear. His sole aim appeared to be to save his life. He appealed to Captain Tumlinson, as a Mason, to save him. Captain Tumlinson claimed that he was not present just then, but I saw him soon afterwards.

"Helm's party went to San Patricio from Choate's, but parties were continually lurking about the neighborhood for a week, which kept the neighborhood in a state of anxious suspense. I was six weeks confined to bed, unable to help myself at all. But, thank God, I have lived to see such things done away with.

"Crockett Choate was killed about three hundred yards from the house."

On the 23rd of November in 1869, a group of Regulators arrived at the ranch of W. B. Morris in McMullen County. There they captured Morris' son-in-law, Martin Taylor, whom they had been chasing. McMullen County had no court or jailhouse, so the Regulators set out with Taylor and Morris bound for the jail at Oakville in Live Oak County. The bullet-riddled bodies of Taylor and Morris were discovered the following day along that route.

When Edmund J. Davis took oath as governor of Texas in 1870, the here-to-fore quasi-legal Regulators no longer had the blessing of the state's highest office. It wasn't necessarily because Governor Davis was more ethical than former Governor Reynolds. He simply wanted control of the state's military

Governor Edmund J. Davis organized the highly unpopular Texas State Police. *Texas State Library & Archives Commission (Photograph of a painting by William Henry Huddle)*

forces. With the loosely-knit Texas Rangers (temporarily) disbanded, Davis was instrumental in organizing the Texas State Police, which would become a highly unpopular organization. Jack Helm was one of four captains named to the new force. Many of the officers recruited by Helm were former members of his old group of Regulators. Two of these were Jim Cox and Joe Tumlinson who were very anti-Taylor. Another of Helm's key comrades was Bill Sutton. Sutton was hated by the Taylors. Buck Taylor and a fellow named Dick Chisholm had been shot to death outside a Clinton saloon on Christmas eve in 1868 following a disagreement with Bill Sutton. Buck Taylor had just returned from driving a herd of horses to market in east Texas. Evidently, part of the herd consisted of some Sutton horses which Taylor included in the drive (for a fee). When he later found out that Sutton's horses had been stolen, Buck confronted Bill and called him a horse thief. Sutton and his compadres were never brought to trial.

Several months prior to the incident at Clinton, Bill Sutton shot and killed a suspected horse thief named Charley Taylor. The shooting occurred in Bastrop on the 25th of March. Charley Taylor may or may not have been kin to the Taylors of the area. If he was, the relationship was distant.

The DeWitt County Taylors indicated that they were not related to Charley Taylor, and possibly did so because he was a suspected horse thief. Two years earlier an incident occurred that may indicate otherwise, however. Charley Taylor shot a fellow named Polk whose wounded body was taken to the house of a Regulator, Captain John Littleton. He is the same Littleton that later set out to get Hays and Doboy Taylor stating, "I will do it or die." As previously mentioned, he and his comrade Stannard turned up dead.

Pitkin Taylor (brother of Creed) married Susan Cochran Day in the first marriage recorded in DeWitt County history. The couple had three children—a child who died at birth, Jim and Amanda. Additionally, Susan had three children from her prior marriage to Robert Day—John, Will and Betty. Amanda Taylor and Betty Day married brothers, Henry and William Kelly respectfully. They all

Pitkin Taylor and his wife Susan. At Pitkin's funeral their son Jim vowed to wash his "... hands in old Bill Sutton's blood." *Elizabeth Kelly Brautigam.*

lived in close proximity south of Cuero. Among their neighbors were Wiley and Eugene Kelly, brothers of Henry and William, as well as Susan's sons John and Will Day.

In mid-August of 1870 the Kelly brothers and their families traveled to the community of Sweet Home in Lavaca County to attend the performance of a circus. Apparently unhappy with the show, the Kellys proceeded to shoot out the lights. It was all the excuse Jack Helm and Bill Sutton needed to continue their war against the Taylor clan. Early on the 26th of August, Bill Sutton, Doc White (who had been with Sutton when Charley Taylor was killed), John Meadows and Deputy Simmons (from Hallettsville in Lavaca County) rode to the homes of Henry and William Kelly and arrested the two brothers. With the Kellys, the lawmen set out on the road to Hallettsville. Amanda Taylor took a buggy and picked up her mother-in-law Delilah Kelly, with the intent of riding with the group to Lavaca County. In an obvious effort to lose the women, Sutton and his bunch took a "shortcut" through the brush whereby a wagon would be incapable of following.

In a later statement sworn before a Justice of the Peace, Amanda Taylor told how she saw her husband and brother-in-law killed in cold blood. She indicated that she had climbed from her buggy and ascended a rise overlooking the trail through the brush which the group had taken. She stated that the posse had stopped forty or fifty yards away and that John Meadows was no longer with them. William Kelly had dismounted and was attempting to light his pipe when Bill Sutton shot him. Instantly, Doc White shot Amanda's husband, Henry, and he toppled from his horse. The court later upheld the plea of the lawmen that they had shot the prisoners while in the act of attempting to escape. There was a huge public outcry following the Kelly murders. State Senator Bolivar Pridgen of Prices Creek in DeWitt County was extremely vocal about the killings. He condemned Jack Helm and the State Police for their methods. Newspapers across the state attacked the actions of Governor Davis. He felt the heat, which eventually resulted in the dismissal of Jack Helm from the State Police. This ouster had little effect on the citizens of DeWitt County, however, as Jack Helm still held the office of sheriff.

Doboy Taylor had "disappeared" for a while. He resurfaced in Kerrville in late 1871. With Jack Helm removed from the State Police force and C. S. Bell having moved out of the vicinity, Doboy could breathe easier. He applied for a position as agent for a cattle buying firm. When the firm hired Sim Holstein for the position, Doboy became incensed. From the gate outside Holstein's hotel, Doboy called the new agent out. The conversation over the gate became bitter.

According to the San Antonio *Express*, on December 13, 1871:

> "Suddenly Taylor drew his pistol and fired at Holstein but overshot him—Holstein sprang over the gate, and before Taylor could shoot again, wrested his pistol from him and felled him to the ground with it. Taylor regained his feet, but was immediately shot down a second and third time. Then Taylor ran toward his house, calling on his friends for assistance. Another shot from Holstein brought him to the ground. His friends were prevented from doing anything by the determined attitude of Holstein. Taylor . . . survived six hours and died at 11 o'clock the same night. He was sensible to the last, and spent his last hours imprecating and cursing the man he had attempted to murder."

Sim Holstein, unarmed when he approached the gate, was obviously a very tough individual.

One night (possibly September of 1872) Pitkin Taylor heard the bell of one of his oxen out in the cornfield. In his nightshirt he stepped outside to see if one of the oxen had wandered into his corn. As he did so, several shots rang out and Pitkin Taylor slumped to the ground. Pitkin, who was badly wounded, was moved to Lavaca County for safety. He lived for about six months, then died in March of 1873. According to the Taylor-Day-Kelly version of the story, Bill Sutton and four henchmen removed the bell from one of the oxen, slipped into the cornfield, and then rattled the bell with the certainty that Taylor would step outside.

Alfred Hays Day's account of Pitkin Taylor's funeral is as follows:

> "It was a grim and tragic scene. The burial plot was near the river on a shaded knoll. Around the open grave the relatives of the murdered man were assembled. Among the mourners were young Jim Taylor, son of the deceased, and five other youthful kin of the slain man. In hideous contrast to this grief-stricken group, across the river while the funeral services were being conducted Bill Sutton assembled his cut throat [sic] gang in bold mockery. With raw drink and coarse jest and wild firing of guns they celebrated the death of Pitkin Taylor while he was being lowered into the grave.
>
> "Hearing this hilarity, Jim's mother, who had borne up well under her grief, broke down and wept. If there had ever been a doubt in young Jim's mind what he should do about the slaying of his father, it was cleared up then. If ever a man was provoked into taking the law into his own hands Jim Taylor was justly provoked; if ever a man had reason to see that Justice was

meted out, Jim Taylor was inspired by that reason.

"Putting his arm protectingly about his mother, he vowed to her: 'Do not weep mother [sic]. I will wash my hands in old Bill Sutton's blood!' The five other youthful relatives likewise pledged themselves to the same cause."

Bill Sutton was sitting in Bank's Saloon and Billiard Parlor at Cuero one Friday night when someone attempted to take his life. Two shots were fired into the building from the outside. One of the slugs penetrated Sutton's arm and side, wounding the lawman. On another occasion, Sutton and a few comrades were riding toward Clinton when they were ambushed. One of the men was wounded in the leg, and three of their horses were slain. No one knows who participated in either attack. We do know, however, that Bill Sutton was number one on the Taylor hit list.

John Wesley Hardin was one of the most dangerous gunfighters on the western frontier. In fact, he was probably involved in more gunfights than any other individual. In his autobiography, Hardin claims to have disposed of 44 men, but then he was known to be a braggart. About 25 percent of those deaths are verifiable through county records and documents. Many deaths, however, went unrecorded in those days. By the year 1871, eighteen-year-old Wes Hardin had already gained quite a reputation. As Hardin was being transported by the State Police from Marshall to Waco to stand trial (for a murder he had not committed), he killed a guard named Jim Smolly and escaped. Wes Hardin fled to Gonzales County to seek refuge at the ranch of his cousins, the Clements, south of the town of Smiley. He worked as a cowpoke and attempted to maintain a low profile. But Wes couldn't stay out of trouble. During the following year he was involved in several shootings, was wounded twice and was also captured. Wes' cousin, Emmanuel "Manning" Clements, broke Hardin out of the Gonzales jail (in October of 1872) by slipping a file to Wes which he used to cut the window bars. Clements then returned and pulled Hardin through the opening with his lariat.

In April of 1873 at Cuero, Wes Hardin became involved in an argument with J. B. Morgan, a deputy of Jack Helm. There is a possibility that Morgan may have attempted to arrest Hardin while he was having a drink in a local saloon. Wes walked out of the saloon with Morgan in pursuit. As Morgan drew his revolver, Hardin whirled and shot the deputy in the head. Shortly after this incident, the Taylor faction gained some valuable recruits—Wes Hardin; Manning Clements; his brothers Gibson, Jim and Joe; and Gibson's brother-in-law George Tennelle.

John Wesley Hardin in 1871 at the age of 18. When this photograph was taken in Abilene, Hardin was already a seasoned gunfighter.
Kansas State Historical Society.

Shortly thereafter, Jack Helm led a large posse to Gonzales County, and the Clement's ranch, in search of Wes Hardin. The men were away rounding up strays, but Sheriff Helm succeeded in frightening Jane Bowen Hardin, Wes' new wife, and the Clements women. Incensed by the posse's visit, Wes Hardin, Manning Clements and George Tennelle met with Jim, John and Scrap Taylor. They decided it was time to wage all-out war on Sutton, Helm, Cox, Tumlinson and the others. They wasted no time in taking the offensive.

On the 16th of June in 1873, Bill Sutton set out for Clinton to testify in the Bank's Saloon and Billiard Parlor shooting at Cuero on the 1st of April. Sutton was still recovering from his wounds, so he rode in a buggy. He was accompanied by Doc White, John Meadows, Horace French and Ad Patterson who were on horseback. Midway between Sutton's home and Clinton the group was ambushed. Meadows took a slug in one leg and French's horse was slain. There was no further damage. Feeling the heat, William and Laura Sutton moved to Victoria to get further away from the fighting.

Scrap Taylor, an active participant in the feud, would often run with Alf Day and Jim Taylor. *Elizabeth Kelly Brautigam*

One day in June of 1873, Jim Cox, Joe Tumlinson, H. Ragland and Jake Cresman were returning from the courthouse at Helena in Karnes County, where Cox was under indictment and had to answer certain charges. Tumlinson, who was his neighbor, Cresman and Ragland apparently went along for the ride. When the party reached the San Antonio River Tumlinson and Ragland opted for a different crossing than Cox and Cresman. It probably saved their lives. Jim Taylor, Scrap Taylor, Alf Day and Bud Dowlearn (whose mother was formerly a Taylor by marriage) were hidden awaiting the approach of the others. Suddenly a volley of gunfire erupted. The lifeless bodies of Jim Cox and Jake Cresman toppled from their horses. It is said that there were 19 buckshot wounds in Cox's body. Tumlinson and Ragland were far enough from the shooting that they were able to flee.

During the last week of July in 1873 Wes Hardin and Jim Taylor were at a blacksmith shop in Albuquerque, Texas where Hardin was having his horse shod. Jack Helm, and a few friends, spotted Jim Taylor and made a beeline to the blacksmith shop. Hearing the negative tone of the approaching voices, Hardin grabbed his shotgun and fired at Sheriff Helms. The blast scored a direct hit. Jim Taylor put several slugs in Helms' head to assure that he was dead. With Hardin's shotgun aimed directly at them, Helms' cohorts refused to participate in the action.

The Taylors received word that there was a large gathering of men at Joe Tumlinson's place. Realizing that the Sutton faction might be amassing for an attack, the Taylors decided to surprise them first. The Taylors, including Wes Hardin, crept toward the Tumlinson residence at approximately 2 a.m. They intended to get close to the porch where many men were sleeping, then open fire. Tumlinson's dogs detected the Taylors, however, and began barking loudly awakening the Sutton men who quickly took cover. Sporadic fire occurred throughout the siege which began early Tuesday morning and lasted until the sheriff and a large contingency of citizens talked the feuding parties into a truce sometime after daybreak on Wednesday. It was agreed that the principal members of each faction should accompany the sheriff to Clinton where a formal truce could be drawn up and signed. Both parties agreed, and the other participants were allowed to disperse and head toward their respective homes. The following account of this event occurred in the *Gonzales Enquirer* and was reprinted in the *Houston Telegraph*:

> "It is with no little gratification that we record a cessation of hostilities between the above name beligerents. It appears from the facts as related to us by a responsible party, that on Monday night last Wesley Hardin, accompanied with some 35 or 40 men, well armed, marched to the residence of Joe Tumlinson, in DeWitt County, surrounded his house and held him in seige for two nights and one day. In the meantime Joe Tumlinson and party, numbering 15 men, and strongly fortified, managed to dispatch a courier to Clinton for the sheriff to hasten to his assistance. After summoning about 50 men the sheriff started for the 'seat of war', where he arrived on Wednesday morning and found Hardin's men formed in line of battle. A brief conference with the parties revealed the unexpected but agreeable intelligence that a compromise had been effected between Hardin and Tumlinson; in other words, a treaty of peace had been agreed upon, and the two parties were ready to proceed to Clinton, a distance of 16 miles, and sign documents to that effect. The

line of march was at once taken up. Hardin's men leading the column, the Sheriff's posse following, and Tumlinson's party bringing up the rear. Arriving at Clinton, Hardin halted on one side of the town, and Tumlinson on the other, while the sheriff's men marched directly into the town. After signing the documents and having the same recorded in the Clerk's Office, both parties quietly dispersed to the intense gratification of the law-abiding and peace-loving citizens."

In the Old West, it was rare when feudists adhered to the terms of a truce. This one lasted about four months before guns were blazing again. In late December, Wiley Pridgen (brother of ex-senator Bolivar Pridgen) was gunned down by unknown assassins near the entrance to Jim Pridgen's store in Thomaston. Several accounts have been given as to who the murderers might be, but nobody knew for certain. The Taylor faction, however, was sure that Bill Sutton was involved. The Taylors cornered Bill Sutton and some of his friends at the courthouse in Clinton. Realizing that their community might quickly become a battleground, Judge Henry Clay Pleasants and several of the town's women approached the Taylors and prevailed upon them to carry their feud elsewhere. They didn't want Clinton's citizens endangered or the town shot up. The Taylors agreed to take their fight elsewhere and hit the road to Cuero. Sutton and his men followed. Sutton sent a request for help to Joe Tumlinson, and then holed up at the Gulf Hotel in Cuero. Tumlinson arrived with reinforcements and yet another siege wound up in a stalemate. Once again, both parties agreed to sign a truce—and they did. Although the newspapers voiced optimism, nobody really expected the feudists to adhere to this armistice either—and they didn't.

During the next few weeks three more men died, and another was wounded. One of the slain men was Bolivar Pridgen's ex-slave, Abraham Pickens (who had continued to work for Pridgen). Supposedly, Pickens was killed because he would not divulge Bolivar's whereabouts. Abraham's clothes were filled with rocks and his body was thrown into the river.

Word filtered through Bolivar Pridgen to Jim Taylor that Bill Sutton and his wife Laura were preparing to leave Texas via a ship departing from the port at Indianola. Joe Hardin (Wes' brother) and his cousin Alec Barrickman, both of whom were from Comanche, were visiting in DeWitt County. Wes Hardin persuaded Joe and Alec to snoop around (as they would not be recognized) to see what information they might obtain. They discovered that Bill and Laura Sutton were scheduled to depart on March 11, bound for the port at New Orleans. Jim and Bill Taylor followed the others to Indianola. Bill was a grandson of William Riley Taylor (brother of Jim's dad, Pitkin) and was therefore Jim's second cousin. Shortly

Bill and Laura Sutton. Following the death of Bill Sutton, his wife, Laura, offered a reward for the capture of Jim Taylor. *The Center for American History, University of Texas at Austin.*

after noon on the 11th of March in 1874, Bill Sutton, his friend Gabriel Slaughter and Bill's pregnant wife Laura were standing on the ship's deck waiting for the crew to cast off. Jim and Bill Taylor quickly approached. Jim Taylor shot Bill Sutton in the head and heart. Bill Taylor also fired and his slug hit Gabriel Slaughter in the head. Sutton and Slaughter were both dead as they fell at the feet of a distraught Laura Sutton. Before the Taylors fled, Jim seized Bill Sutton's ivory-handled revolver. Following this incident Laura Sutton offered a personal reward of $1,000 for the arrest of Jim Taylor (who already had a $500 bounty on his head).

The Taylors escaped to the house of Bolivar Pridgen in Thomaston, where the news was received with great joy. Pridgen had his cook prepare a lavish meal to celebrate the occasion. Jim Taylor helped Wes Hardin prepare a herd for its drive north. They decided to spend a few days in Comanche, then reunite with the drovers at some point on the trail. Bill Taylor decided to lie low in Texas.

Bill Taylor didn't lie low enough, however, and was arrested by Reuben Brown, the city marshal of Cuero. Taylor was transported to the jail at Galveston to await trial.

While in Comanche, Wes Hardin wagered on some horse races and won heavily. It was a nice present for his twenty-first birthday. His mood turned sour, however, when he learned that Charles Webb, deputy sheriff of nearby Brown County, was in Comanche with the intention of killing Hardin and collecting the $1800 reward on his head. Wes was at Jack Wright's Saloon when Webb found him. Hardin offered to buy Webb a drink at the bar. As Charles Webb stepped toward the bar, he drew his revolver and fired. Alertly, Hardin jumped to one side as he drew his own pistol. Webb's bullet grazed Hardin who fired. His slug ripped through the deputy's head. Although he was already dead, as he fell, Bud Dixon (Wes' cousin) and Jim Taylor also shot him. They immediately fled the scene. A large and irate mob could not find Hardin and Taylor but were successful in capturing Bud Dixon. They also rounded up Joe Hardin and Tom Dixon (neither of whom were directly involved in the killing of Sheriff Webb). The three were locked up in the Comanche jail. Several days later an angry mob dragged the trio from the jailhouse and lynched them. Joe Hardin's cousin Alec Barrickman and Ham Anderson (two of Wes' stock hands) decided to hide at the house of Bill Stone. Barrickman and Anderson were discovered by a posse and shot to death. Another posse rode to Mason County where Hardin's drovers were holding his cattle. Three or four of the cowboys escaped. Doc Brosius (Hardin's trail boss), Scrap Taylor, Kute Tuggle and Jim White were taken into custody and escorted to DeWitt County. During the night of June 20, 1874, a mob broke the prisoners out of jail. Brosius was somehow rescued by a fellow Mason during all the commotion. The others were hanged from a tree near the Clinton cemetery.

The hunt for Taylor men continued. A posse cornered George Tennelle at the residence of John Runnel in Gonzales County. When Tennelle refused to surrender, he was shot to death by the posse.

The reward for John Wesley Hardin had been raised to $4,000. He felt the heat and knew it was time to leave Texas. He sent word to Jane who met him in New Orleans, and the couple then relocated to Pollard, Escambia County, Alabama where they stayed with friends (the Whitings) and assumed the aliases of Mr. and Mrs. J. H. Swain.

By this time, Richard Coke had become governor, the State Police had been dissolved and the Texas Rangers rode once again. Citizens of DeWitt County pleaded with Governor Coke to maintain a detachment of Texas Rangers in the area as a peacekeeping force. He agreed to do so. In late July, Captain

Leander H. McNelly led a force of forty Rangers into DeWitt County. McNelly was a tough individual who had an advanced case of tuberculosis (called consumption in those days), and he knew he was dying. It was probably the reason that he had no fear. McNelly's force maintained a highly visible profile and things began to settle down in the area.

Bolivar Pridgen was successful in obtaining indictments against Joe Tumlinson and 26 other men for the murder of his employee, Abraham Pickens. Joe Tumlinson died of natural causes before he could be tried. It was probably for that reason that the case against the others never came to trial.

After two postponements, Bill Taylor's trial was scheduled for September of 1875. He was transported from Galveston to the jail at Indianola a few days before his case was to be heard. During the interim, a severe hurricane struck Indianola. As the Gulf surge raised the water level in Matagorda Bay, the Indianola jailhouse began to fill with water. Concerned that the prisoners (Taylor, two rustlers and a rapist) might drown, District Attorney Bill Crain released them, and the five men made their way to the second floor of the courthouse which was adjacent to the jail. That day, and the next, Bill Taylor and another prisoner named Blackburn joined in the rescue effort. Many people were saved due to the heroism of Taylor and Blackburn. After two days, the savage winds finally subsided. The death toll

Indianola, Texas, as it looked prior to the hurricane of 1875. The view is looking west down Main Street. *Texas State Library & Archives Commission.*

was large. Sheriff Fred Busch arrived on horseback (the 17th of September) and entered the courthouse to talk with the nearly 100 survivors who had found shelter there. During an unsuspecting moment, Blackburn snatched Busch's revolver from its holster. While holding the sheriff at gunpoint, Blackburn appropriated the lawman's horse. Blackburn and Bill Taylor mounted the animal and raced out of town.

Two months later to the day, City Marshal Reuben Brown was dealing Monte in the Exchange Saloon at Cuero when a few men walked in and shot him to death. Two black men at Brown's table were wounded as well. Although no charges were ever filed, it is believed that the responsible party consisted of Jim Taylor, Bill Taylor, Joe Bennett and possibly two others. The murder was obviously a retaliation for Brown's arrest of Bill Taylor following the killing of Bill Sutton. A few weeks later Bill Taylor and Joe Bennett were ambushed by unknown assailants near the town of Clinton. Bennett received a superficial wound before the pair escaped to safety.

On December 27, 1875, Jim Taylor and a large party of armed men rode into Clinton. Their purpose was uncertain, but Sheriff Weisiger was convinced that they planned to burn down the courthouse. Weisiger recruited the help of several citizens who were determined to defend the courthouse. Two members of the Taylor bunch were Tom King and his adopted brother Ed Davis. Their father, Martin King, owned the blacksmith shop and livery stable in Clinton. While most of the Taylor men remained on the outskirts of town, Jim Taylor, Mace Arnold (who was known as Winchester Smith) and J. G. Hendrix stabled their horses at King's livery. Meanwhile, Weisiger sent a boy named Charley Page to Cuero to request the assistance of Deputy Sheriff Dick Hudson. Hudson rounded up a posse of Sutton sympathizers which included Kit Hunter (a cousin of the deceased Bill Sutton).

Sheriff Weisiger advised Martin King that a posse was on its way. Weisiger stated that a fight was certain and that King's sons would be in grave danger. The sheriff told him that his sons' lives would be spared if he would agree to help the law by locking up those horses which the Taylor gang had left at his stable. Fearing for the lives of his sons, Martin King agreed to do so.

As the posse rode in, the Taylor men who were in town scampered to reach their horses only to find that they had been locked up. Jim Taylor, Winchester Smith and Hendrix dashed through Martin King's house in an effort to reach a log building situated in an orchard. Suddenly Taylor was confronted by Kit Hunter. Simultaneously, they exchanged shots. Taylor's bullet went through Hunter's hat while Hunter's slug shattered Taylor's right arm. By then, a barrage of bullets were flying at the Taylor men from different directions. Jim Taylor and Winchester Smith were killed. Hendrix was wounded and would soon die. It all happened so fast that those members of the Taylor bunch waiting on the outskirts of town were never able to help. They departed in haste. Martin King's sons were arrested and jailed.

Martin King was a marked man for betraying the Taylors. One night several months later, a volley of gunfire killed Martin King in the doorway of Dola Davis' saloon. A slug from the gun of one of the assassins wounded Davis in the leg during the attack.

In early 1876, a posse arrived at the residence of A. J. Allen, a member of the Taylor gang. The Henderson County sheriff advised Allen that they had a warrant for his arrest. Allen refused to submit to arrest, and a fight broke out in which a deputy was killed. Allen was severely wounded and would eventually die. Another man was wounded as well.

Once again, Captain McNelly and his Texas Rangers camped in DeWitt County. Their mere presence minimized trouble.

An incident that was peripheral to the Sutton-Taylor feud occurred on the night of September 19, 1876. Dr. Philip Brassell, a civic-minded citizen, and his son George, a Taylor sympathizer, were forced from their home by a posse—and were then murdered on the road a short distance from their home. Eight posse members were arrested and jailed by the Texas Rangers. Seven members of the posse (which included Bill Cox, a son of Jim Cox) spent years in and out of courtrooms. There were indictments, trials, changes of venue, acquittals, more indictments, more trails, convictions, appeals, more acquittals, another conviction and pardon (and not necessarily in that order). Eventually, all of the accused men walked free.

Bill Taylor remained a fugitive until April 15, 1877, when he was arrested in Coleman by the Texas Rangers. Taylor was taken to the jail at Austin. In late August, he was reunited with John Wesley Hardin. Hardin had been arrested in Pensacola, Florida, on the 23rd of August and was then transported to Austin to await trial for the murder of Sheriff Charles Webb at Comanche. Hardin was found guilty and sentenced to the penitentiary at Huntsville. Bill Taylor was transferred to the jail at Galveston in order to stand trial at Indianola. Following a change of venue to the court at Texanna (which at the time was the county seat of Jackson County), Taylor was acquitted in the killing of Bill Sutton. It was a blow for the prosecution which now asked for a delay in the murder trial of Gabriel Slaughter, obviously with the hope of preparing a better case. A delay was allowed. Taylor was granted a Writ of Habeas Corpus and was able to post bail in the amount of $5,000 which was secured by Bolivar Pridgen, John Taylor, Eugene Kelly and Rice S. Flournoy. Following another continuance, the prosecuting attorney asked for a dismissal of the case. Bill Taylor was a free man.

The bloody Sutton-Taylor feud, which for years had terrorized the citizens of several Texas counties, finally came to an end.

Belton, the county seat of Bell County, as it looked after the Civil War. *Collection of the Bell County Museum.*

REPRISAL IN BELL COUNTY

During the Civil War there were many communities scattered across the western frontier that lacked adequate protection. While most of the young men were off fighting battles, security was often left to older men and young boys. Sometimes they would organize a protection agency to help guard the home front. Such was the case with the Home Guard in Bell County, Texas. Ethics wasn't a strong suit for many Bell County ranchers. Some used the Home Guard as a screen for rustling activities. On a wide-open range it was easy to round up strays that belonged to neighbors who were on a battlefield far away. Upon returning home, some of the owners would "steal" their cattle and horses back. Much hostility grew out of the rustling activity.

The Home Guard was led by John Early, an individual of dubious character who seemed to enjoy the sport of dragging deserters from their hideouts in the rugged bush country to the west. When the war ended, Early's house became headquarters for scalawags and carpetbaggers. Among his cohorts were Republican Dr. Calvin Clark, considered a turncoat by many, and Judge Hiram Christian, leader of the carpetbaggers. The three men, and their circle of friends, were highly disliked by the majority of Bell County citizens—Southern sympathizers, former soldiers of the Confederate States of America, and their kinfolk.

Sam Hasley was a Confederate soldier who carried a huge grudge against John Early. It began prior to the war's end. In early 1865, John Early and members of the Home Guard captured three deserters who were on the run. Accompanied by their prisoners, the group made camp near a place called Reed's

Lake. Two companies of Confederate soldiers also pitched camp nearby. The fugitives were secured before Early and his bunch retired for the night. The following morning, the Home Guard awoke to find the deserters hanging by their necks from a pecan tree.

Whether, or not, there was any justification in John Early's actions during the aftermath of the hangings is a question which will probably never be answered. Early singled out several locals, went to their homes, quizzed them, badgered them, then pushed them around. One of the citizens who was on the receiving end was Sam Hasley's father, Drew. Early shoved Drew Hasley around, then jerked a handful of hair from his white beard.

Sam Hasley was not one to rush right into a fight. He was cool, calm, and calculating. When he returned from the war to find that his father had been insulted and mistreated, he vowed retaliation. It was some time before an opportunity arose. One night, while riding on a desolate road, Sam Hasley encountered a group of scalawags who were traveling in the opposite direction. As he passed the column of riders the white face of the last horse stood out in the moonlight. Hasley realized it was Early's horse. As they neared each other Hasley spurred his mount, fired point-blank at Early, then raced out of sight. When Hasley heeled his mount it caused Early's horse to shy. When it did, Hasley's bullet struck the horse. The horse died and Early was unscathed. Early, Christian and Clark decided that it was time to make an example out of some prominent Southerners in Bell County. He used the lynching of the deserters as an excuse to do so. A detachment of soldiers arrested several people, including Drew Hasley, and escorted them to the jail at Austin. It was the last straw as far as Sam Hasley was concerned.

Lawlessness in Bell County had never been greater. Not only did the authorities take advantage of the citizens, but horse thieves and cattle rustlers were running rampant. The citizens of Bell County finally took matters into their own hands. A group of vigilantes emerged. Their moves were highly calculated and they executed them to precision. Furthermore, they were masters at covering their tracks. The vigilantes moved swiftly. Six previously dreaded outlaws met their demise in April of 1866. In June, the bodies of two more horse thieves were found floating in the river near Three Forks.

Speculation has it that the vigilantes were composed predominately of former Confederate soldiers, and that their leaders were Sam Hasley and his brother-in-law Jim McRae. Whoever they were, their identities were highly protected.

While working at the courthouse on the 2nd of July, Judge Hiram Christian somehow found out that he was a marked man. That night, under the cover of darkness, Christian fled Bell County. The vigilantes tracked him all the way to Missouri, where they finally caught up with him. The execution of Hiram Christian was swift, and the vigilantes returned to Texas.

Jonathan and Newton Lindley departed from San Antonio with a warrant for the arrest of two Bell County men whose names were Duncan and Dawes. They were wanted for the murder of Jasper Lindley, one of the horse thieves who had been found in the river near Three Forks. Jonathan, who was Jasper's father, and Newton were accompanied by fifteen soldiers when they arrived in Bell County. Confident of their innocence, Duncan and Dawes surrendered to the soldiers and the group headed toward San Antonio. Before they had traveled far, Jonathan Lindley shot the two prisoners out of their saddles. He and Newton then fled the scene.

Jonathan and Newton Lindley were captured and escorted to the Bell County jail where they were locked up. While they were awaiting trial, a mob surrounded the jailhouse and then shot and killed the prisoners. Naturally, nobody recognized any members of the mob, nor did anybody "discover" the bodies any time soon.

David Griffin was a brother-in-law of Jim McRae, who, as we have previously mentioned, was a brother-in-law of Sam Hasley. The Hasley, McRae and Griffin clans were suspected as being the core of the vigilantes. While Sam Hasley stepped softly and took a low profile, Jim McRae was bold and blatant, and a more visible leader. McRae had become John Early's number one target. On July 30, 1869, Early and a posse approached the Griffin residence where a party was in progress. The Griffins, McRaes and Hasleys were having a festive time. Fearing that a confrontation would endanger the women and children Early withdrew his men a short distance back down the road. Before long Jim McRae and David Griffin rode up the trail in the direction of the concealed posse members. As the two riders drew near, Early and his men shot McRae out of the saddle. Griffin whirled his mount and fled. The badly wounded McRae was able to discharge a couple of shots and wounded a posse member named McDaniels. Jim McRae died later that evening.

Following McRae's death the vigilantes broke up and dispersed. Eight months later, a telegram was received which announced that ". . . Calvin Clark of Bell County, Texas was killed in Arkansas by a desperado named Halsey [sic] who followed him from Texas."

John Early disappeared. Could he also have met his demise by the hand of Sam Hasley? We may never know.

Billy the Kid (William H. Bonney, Henry McCarty, or Kid Antrim) as photographed outside Beaver Smith's Saloon, at Fort Sumner, about 1879. *Western History Collections, University of Oklahoma Library.*

THE LINCOLN COUNTY WAR AND BILLY THE KID

At the First Presbyterian Church at Santa Fe, New Mexico, on March 1, 1873, wedding vows were exchanged between William Henry Harrison Antrim and Catherine McCarty. Among the witnesses were Catherine's two sons, Joseph (who was called Josie), and Henry (who was possibly thirteen-years-old). This is the first substantial documentation we have as to the life of Henry McCarty (otherwise known at various times as Henry Antrim, William Antrim, Kid Antrim, William H. Bonney, Billy the Kid, or simply the Kid). Henry may have been the son of a McCarty—possibly even a Bonney (illegitimate or legitimate). Regardless of those years which are shrouded in mystery, Henry was destined to become legendary.

Shortly after the wedding, the Antrims moved to Silver City, New Mexico, where William prospected and Catherine took in boarders to supplement their income. Catherine died of tuberculosis on September 16, 1874, just a year and a half after their wedding. Henry was, as his teacher and others later indicated, a helpful child who was no more of a problem than any other boy his age. He was a jovial lad as well, who always had a good sense of humor.

The Kid's first scrape with the law resulted from a petty theft of clothes from Charlie Sun, a Chinese laundryman. He was locked up in the Silver City jail. The Kid couldn't stand the idea of being confined, and after only two nights behind bars escaped by wiggling through a chimney. Kid Antrim fled to Arizona Territory where he spent much of the next two years as a cowhand, rustler, thief, and part-time gambler. Twice he was arrested for larceny, but the guardhouse at Camp Grant couldn't hold him, and twice he escaped. Why he didn't flee the area is a question for speculation, but he remained in the vicinity to get into even bigger trouble—murder.

On August 17, 1877, at Bonita, near Camp Grant, the Kid scuffled with an Irishman named Frank Cahill. Cahill grabbed him. The Irishman had picked on Antrim before, but this time the Kid decided that enough was enough. He drew and shot Cahill through the stomach, mortally wounding him. This time Antrim fled the scene. He headed back to New Mexico Territory, where he continued to run stolen horses, this time for John W. Kinney, who was known as "King of the Rustlers." It is presumably at this time that the Kid first met, then joined up with Jessie Evans and the Boys, the gang of rustlers that operated out of Kinney's ranch outside La Mesilla. They were so brash that they had been known to sell cattle before they were ever rustled. Evans and the Boys ran rampant through southeastern New Mexico, and as they were feared by most, nobody attempted to stop them. That is, until newspaperman Col. Albert J. Fountain founded the *Mesilla Valley Independent*, in which he lambasted the Boys. He offered the Boys twelve ropes and twelve cottonwood trees if room could not be found for them in the county jail. On behalf of the Boys, Evans sent word to Fountain that they planned to kill him on sight. When Governor S. B. Axtell was telegraphed for help, he responded. In short order things became too hot for Jessie Evans and the Boys in Doña Ana County. They decided on a change of scenery and headed to Lincoln County. Whether the Kid accompanied the Boys to Lincoln County, or not, is uncertain. The Kid and Jessie Evans both resurfaced there, ultimately with opposing factions in what was to become known as the Lincoln County War.

The "House" was located at the western end of Lincoln's only street. It was the largest civilian structure in Lincoln County, and headquarters for L. G. Murphy & Company. It was also a store, a saloon, a bunkhouse, and even a Masonic Hall. Lawrence Gustave Murphy and James Joseph Dolan were a shrewd and powerful partnership. Dolan was so close to Murphy that many mistakenly thought him to be an adopted son. Through the House they held a virtual monopoly over Lincoln County's trade. Most of the juicy government contracts for supplying beef to Indian reservations and military posts were controlled by the House, as well. Murphy and Dolan were aided in this effort by cohort John Henry Riley. The financial power of the House regulated much of the cattle flow in the region. It held the reins to the sheriff's office as well.

With the flip of a coin we see the other side. The large cattle ranchers believed that merchants, with little experience in raising cattle, should have no

Lawrence Gustave Murphy (right) and James Joseph Dolan (left) controlled much of the economy in Lincoln County.
Lincoln County Heritage Trust.

control over government contracts, and that the beef suppliers should be able to deal directly with the government. John Henry Tunstall, or the "Englishman" as he was usually called, had an ambition to pocket half of every dollar spent in Lincoln County. He presumed that with his cattle ranch, a store to compete effectively with the House, a bank from which he would make loans to all of the small ranchers (making them all indebted to him), one of his pawns as Indian agent, and the genius of lawyer Alexander Anderson McSween, he could realize his ambition. Though not as rich, McSween (called Mac by his friends) was equally ambitious. He wanted position and money, and was spurred toward that end by his wife Susan E. McSween. Cattle baron, John Simpson Chisum, was fighting his own private "war," but would soon join the Tunstall-McSween faction. The Kid signed on with John Tunstall as a hand—and a gun. By now he was using the name William H. Bonney, or Billy. Billy the Kid was to be very loyal to Tunstall, and would be in the Lincoln County War through its duration. Jimmy Dolan and John Riley assumed command of the House, as L. G. Murphy became terminally ill. Accusations and litigation were followed by more accusations and more litigation. Tensions grew as the hatred between Dolan and Riley on one side, and Tunstall and McSween on the other, heightened. On the morning of February 18, 1878, Jimmy Dolan helped select a posse which was instructed to head off John Tunstall, return him and his party to Lincoln, and furthermore to confiscate some of Tunstall's horses as payment for an outstanding debt. Accompanying the posse were Jessie Evans, Tom Hill, and Frank Baker, who were members of the Boys. While descending into a canyon leading to the Ruidoso Valley, Tunstall and his men encountered a flock of turkeys. John Tunstall remained with the horses while the others scattered out over a distance of several hundred yards in pursuit of the flock. Suddenly, a few members of the posse appeared near Tunstall, and he spurred his mount to ride forward and talk with them. As he neared, Buck Morton shot Tunstall in the chest. A second shot from the revolver of Tom Hill crashed into his head.

Following John Tunstall's murder, many "sympathizers" gathered at McSween's house. Another large group consisting of Dolan, Riley, Sheriff William

John Henry Tunstall was ambitious. His goals put him in direct opposition to the House, and eventually cost him his life. *Lincoln County Heritage Trust.*

Brady, and members of the posse assembled at the House (now J. J. Dolan & Company).

Realizing that Sheriff Brady would not arrest Tunstall's killers, McSween had the Kid and Dick Brewer (Tunstall's foreman) furnish sworn affidavits in the presence of Justice of the Peace Wilson. Town Constable, Atanacio Martinez, armed with warrants which had been issued by Wilson, deputized William Bonney and Fred Waite. The trio proceeded to the House in order to arrest those men named in the warrants. At Dolan's place, the three encountered Sheriff Brady and a large party of gunmen which were bolstered by troops from Fort Stanton. Not only did Brady refuse to allow Martinez to make any arrests, but he took the constable, Bonney and Waite into custody and marched them to the jailhouse. Martinez was only detained, but Bonney and Waite remained in jail for twenty-four hours. To add to the humiliation, Brady confiscated the Kid's rifle. There never had been any question about the Kid's allegiance to the Tunstall-McSween faction, but this incident unleashed a new fury and defiance.

Alexander Anderson McSween, a crafty lawyer, assumed control of the anti-House faction following the death of John Tunstall. *Lincoln County Heritage Trust.*

The factions aligned. The small farmers of the Ruidoso and Hondo valleys and the Hispanics to whom Tunstall had extended credit aligned themselves with McSween, as did cattle baron John Chisum for a while. The ranchers from the Seven Rivers area had already been involved in the Pecos War against Chisum, so they naturally allied themselves with Dolan and Riley. Others siding with the House included District Attorney, 3rd Judicial District at Las Cruces, William L. Rynerson; U.S. District Attorney Thomas B. Catron; Sheriff William Brady and his deputies; the Democratic political machine known as "The Santa Fe Ring;" and John Kinney, the "King of the Rustlers."

Still holding warrants for the arrest of Tunstall's killers, and realizing that the only way justice would be served would be to serve it themselves, certain members of the McSween faction formed a heavily armed vigilante group. They called themselves the "Regulators." The group included Dick Brewer, William Bonney, John Middleton, Fred Waite, Josiah (Doc) Scurlock, Charlie Bowdre, Frank

MacNab, Henry Brown, Jim (Big Jim) French, and Sam Smith. Bent on vengeance, and suspecting that the wanted men were holed up at Jim Dolan's cattle camp over on the Pecos, the Regulators headed southeast. The group sighted five men near the Rio Penasco. Two of the men peeled off, but the Regulators chased the other three. A horse gave out, and one of the three went down. The posse ignored him, for the two remaining men were Buck Morton and Frank Baker. The fugitives eventually surrendered. Over strong objections from the Kid, Brewer agreed to take the duo back to Lincoln. The posse stopped at Chisum's ranch, and picked up a hand named William H. McCloskey. As the group rode toward Lincoln, Morton reached over and snatched McCloskey's pistol from its holster, then fired at him point blank, fatally wounding the ranch hand. Morton and Baker then wheeled their horses in an attempt to flee. The Regulators opened fire and gunned them down (according to Frank MacNab's version of the March 8th incident). Buck Morton's back had nine bullet holes in it, which either indicated

Sheriff William Brady, formerly an army captain stationed at Fort Stanton, was a close friend of both L.G. Murphy and Jimmy Dolan and therefore aligned the "law" with the partisanship of the House. *Lincoln County Heritage Trust.*

excellent marksmanship on the part of the Regulators or simply an assassination by the posse knowing that Sheriff Brady would have turned them loose upon their arrival into Lincoln.

At approximately 9:30 a.m., on April 1, 1878, Sheriff Brady emerged from his office with four deputies, Billy Mathews, George Hindman, George Peppin and John (Jack) Long, then headed down the street, presumably to arrest Alexander McSween. As they walked east they were unaware of the impending danger. Prior to dawn, six Regulators had slipped into the corral adjacent to Tunstall's store, and had drilled gun ports in the corral wall. The firing squad consisted of Frank MacNab, Big Jim French, Henry Brown, John Middleton, Fred Waite, and the Kid. Their rifles were ready. As the sheriff and his deputies passed the corral gate, the Regulators opened fire. Sheriff Brady was killed instantly—being hit in the head, back, and side. George Hindman staggered a few steps, then collapsed. He would also die. John Long also took a slug but scampered to safety, as did Mathews and Peppin. A bystander, John Wilson, was wounded by a stray bullet as he worked in his garden to the south. Big Jim French and Billy the Kid ran through the corral gate to Brady's fallen body, either to grab the warrant for McSween's arrest (which they didn't get), or to fetch the Kid's rifle (confiscated earlier) which Brady was carrying. Billy Mathews fired from across the street. As the two scurried back to the corral, a slug nicked Bonney, then hit French in the thigh. The Regulators figured a way to hide Jim French as he was too hurt to ride. The others mounted, then bolted from the corral gate and charged toward the east end of town amidst a volley of gunfire. John Middleton reined-up and briefly returned the deputies' fire, scattering them once again. He then followed the others out of town.

The Regulators had heard that some of the men for whom they were looking were lying low in the Mescalero Apache Indian Reservation, and they decided to flush them out. This time the riders included Dick Brewer, Billy Bonney, Frank MacNab, John Middleton, Charlie Bowdre, Fred Waite, Big Jim French, Henry Brown, Doc Scurlock, George and Frank Coe, John Scroggins, Ignacio Gonzales, and Steve Stephens. The first night out, they camped on the Rinconada. The following morning (April 6th) they rode to Blazer's Mill, about two miles west of Mescalero. Blazer's Mill was a small settlement which had blossomed around the sawmill of Doc Blazer (once a dentist). The Regulators put their horses in the corral, then headed into one of the houses for a meal. Blazer's corral was enclosed by a fence constructed of planks from the sawmill, thereby hiding the horses inside. Had the horses been visible, Andrew L. "Buckshot" Roberts certainly wouldn't have wandered in. Roberts rode with the posse that killed John Tunstall.

The mill of Dr. Joseph Blazer, in a state of deterioration. The settlement at Blazer's Mill was the scene of a gunfight early one afternoon in which Dick Brewer and Andrew "Buckshot" Roberts lost their lives. *Lincoln County Heritage Trust.*

Frank Coe had finished eating first, and went outside where he saw Roberts approaching the house. Coe greeted Roberts, then the two sat down on the porch to chat. Frank Coe informed "Buckshot" Roberts that the Regulators had a warrant for his arrest. Roberts cocked his rifle as it lay in his lap. Realizing that Roberts was outside, Bowdre, Bonney, and George Coe slipped out to help. Suddenly, Bowdre popped around the corner of the house with his revolver in hand and ordered Roberts to get his hands in the air. Roberts comment was, "Not much, Mary Ann," and the two fired simultaneously. Bowdre's slug hit Roberts in the stomach, while Roberts' nicked Bowdre's gun belt, then hit George Coe in the hand. A second shot hit John Middleton, who was now nearby, in the chest. Badly injured, Roberts stumbled back through the doorway to Doc Blazer's office, and temporary safety. Roberts spotted Blazer's Springfield .45-.60 which he grabbed and quickly loaded with shells stacked nearby. Flattening himself on the floor, he drew a bead through the partially opened doorway. When a head popped up from behind a log pile at the adjacent sawmill, Roberts fired. The shot hit Dick Brewer in the eye, and he fell dead.

Having lost their leader, the discouraged Regulators loaded the two injured men into a wagon and headed toward Fort Stanton. "Buckshot" Roberts died the following afternoon. He and Richard M. Brewer are buried side-by-side at Blazer's Mill.

On the 18th of April, the Grand Jury completed its deliberations on a string

Richard M. Brewer was the first leader of the Regulators. *Lincoln County Heritage Trust.*

of territorial cases. In the murder of John Tunstall, they found indictments against Jessie Evans, George Davis, Frank Rivers (a.k.a. John Long), and Miguel Seguro (Manuel Segovia). James J. Dolan and Jacob (Billy) Mathews were named as accessories. In the murder of Sheriff William Brady and Deputy George Hindman, the jury brought in indictments against William Bonney, John Middleton, Fred Waite, and Henry Brown. Many of the Regulators were indicted in the killing of Andrew Roberts including Charlie Bowdre (who fired the fatal shot), as well as Bonney (this time under the name of Henry Antrim, alias "Kid"), Middleton, Waite, and Brown, among others. James J. Dolan and John H. Riley were indicted for cattle theft. They were asked to leave the county, and they obliged, though they would be heard from again. Furthermore, Alexander McSween was exonerated of charges against him. McSween had won a battle—but not the war. The worst was yet to come.

Frank MacNab, now leader of the Regulators, publicly stated that it was time to clean up the rest of the murderers and rustlers in the Seven Rivers Area.

The Seven Rivers bunch beat MacNab to the punch. A posse of about thirty-five men mounted up and headed for Lincoln. George Peppin, Robert and John Beckwith, Marion Turner, Billy Mathews, Tom Green, and John Long were among the group that included many from the posse that had murdered John Tunstall. On the evening of April 29th, Frank MacNab left Lincoln accompanied by Frank Coe and his partner Ab Saunders. The trio headed toward Coe's farm on the Hondo River. The Seven Rivers bunch spotted the three as they stopped to water their horses. The posse cut loose with a barrage of bullets. MacNab was killed, Saunders wounded, and Coe was allowed to surrender. Under the cover of darkness, the posse filtered into Lincoln. Shooting broke out about 9:00 a.m. on April 30th. The siege continued throughout the day until it was interrupted by troops from Fort Stanton who "escorted" seventeen posse members back to the garrison.

Josiah "Doc" Scurlock was an educated man who loved to read poetry and the classics. He was also a gritty gunfighter. On one occasion, after being shot through his neck, Scurlock killed his adversary. *Lincoln County Heritage Trust.*

The Regulators, with Doc Scurlock now in command, raided the Dolan-Riley cattle camp at Black River on May 14th. Their purpose was to retrieve horses stolen from the Tunstall ranch and others which were the property of Saunders and MacNab. As Scurlock, Bonney, and the others swept in, they killed Manuel Segovia (another member of the posse which killed John Tunstall), Billy Wier, and a teenage boy.

Although Jimmy Dolan was in "exile," he was still active in the Lincoln County War. Making use of his influential friends, who in turn made use of their influential friends, Dolan had John Copeland (a McSween puppet) removed from his post as sheriff of Lincoln County. Law required a new sheriff to post bond as tax collector. With all the commotion at Lincoln, Copeland had failed to do so. Governor Axtell issued a proclamation which removed Copeland and appointed in his place, George W. Peppin, formerly one of Sheriff Brady's deputies, and a friend of the House. The faction which controlled the sheriff's office, had "right" on its side, at least for the time being. On the other side, of course, were the "villains" and "assassins." Dolan had put the wheels into motion for a showdown, but now it was up to Peppin to follow through. Peppin appointed John Long, Marion Turner, Buck Powell, and Jose Chavez y Baca to serve as deputies. He also began to recruit a posse to help serve several outstanding warrants against the Regulators. Alexander McSween fled his home and took refuge with the Regulators, a group which was now growing with the addition of several Hispanics. They avoided near skirmishes with two separate posses, and stayed on the move. They would not be elusive too long, however.

July 14, 1878, was a quiet Sunday in Lincoln. Much of the posse was out of town, down in the San Patricio area. Jimmy Dolan, back in town—and once again calling the shots—was at the Wortley Hotel. He was accompanied by Sheriff Peppin and about five others. John Long, Billy Mathews, and five others occupied the Torreon (Lincoln's defense tower). They were taken completely by surprise when a large group of riders thundered into town, led by Alexander McSween, Billy the Kid, and Doc Scurlock. Each was heavily armed. Once in town, the Regulators scattered. McSween, Bonney, Jim French, and ten other men went straight to, and occupied, McSween's house. Scurlock, Bowdre, Middleton, and ten other men took over Isaac Ellis' store and house. Henry Brown, George Coe, and Sam Smith manned the Tunstall store. Martin Chaves and a sizeable group of Hispanics occupied the Jose Montaño store. The Regulators barricaded windows, drilled holes for gun ports, and settled in for a long siege.

Having been summoned by a rider, Buck Powell led the posse back into

Lincoln. They arrived that evening. Dolan's forces were further bolstered on Monday when John Kinney rode in with some of his ranch hands, and Jessie Evans with a few of the Boys. Most of the Seven Rivers bunch arrived as well. By now, both forces numbered close to fifty.

Sporadic shooting occurred Monday, Tuesday, and Wednesday—through the day, and after dark. Daniel Huff died on Monday. He was hastily buried, and the cause of his death is unknown. On Wednesday, one of Dolan's men, Charlie Crawford, was picked off on a hillside nine hundred yards away by a buffalo gun. He wriggled in agony until Fort Stanton soldiers moved him later in the day. Crawford was to die a week later. W. H. Johnson and two other members of the Dolan faction were wounded. That night, Ben Ellis was shot in the neck while tending to his horses. Thursday brought another day of sporadic shooting.

One month earlier, Congress passed into law the *Posse Comitatus Act*, which prohibited military use of Federal troops in any civil action, unless approved by the President of the United States. Colonel Nathan A. Dudley, commanding officer at Fort Stanton, had his hands tied. Though he tried to disguise the fact, he was openly more sympathetic to the Dolan cause than that of McSween. Thursday evening, Dudley called his officers together to discuss the situation at Lincoln. They supported his decision to "place soldiers in the town of Lincoln for the preservation of the lives of the women and children." On Friday morning, July 19, 1878, he led one company of cavalry into Lincoln. The detachment set up camp directly opposite the Montaño store and house.

The McSween faction had occupied the most strategic locations in town. The diversion and cease fire created by the arrival of the detachment gave Dolan's men an advantage. They were able to move in closer around the McSween house. With a howitzer trained on their front door, Chaves decided to abandon the Montaño store. He moved his men to the Ellis house. Unaware of Dudley's intentions, the McSween faction grew uneasy. When Peppin realized that Chaves and the Hispanics had moved down to the Ellis house, he took a group of men and advanced in that direction. Suddenly, a large group of riders bolted from Ellis' corral with their guns blazing. The group included Scurlock, Bowdre, Middleton, Chaves, and all the men who had been at both Montaño's and Ellis' places. As the group whirled their horses and rode out of town, injuries were inflicted on both sides.

Some of Peppin's possemen gained access to an outside wall of the McSween house and began to pile kindling against the building. Gunfire, which erupted from the hill north of town, attempted to drive the posse back. Scurlock, Chaves, and the others had moved to this new vantage point. When the cavalry trained their howitzer on the hillside, the Regulators disappeared.

Meanwhile, McSween's house had been set on fire by John Long and a fellow known only as Dummy. Henry Brown, George Coe, and Sam Smith (who were now in the grain warehouse behind the Tunstall store) opened fire on Long and Dummy as they retreated from the burning house. In what may have been

Strong-willed Susan Ellen McSween was a driving force behind her husband, Alex. *Lincoln County Heritage Trust.*

the only humorous incident in the Lincoln County War, the two dove into the outhouse and submerged themselves below ground level to avoid the gunfire. Elizabeth Shield, Susan McSween's pregnant sister, ran out and extinguished the flames. The house, however, was torched again, and this time the fire took hold. Gunfire increased, to and from the slowly burning house. Eventually a temporary cease fire was called in order that Susan McSween, Elizabeth Shield, and the children could be evacuated. The blaze illuminated the sky as darkness fell. As the heat intensified, Alexander McSween sat disconsolately. He was out of ideas.

Billy the Kid outlined a plan. He would take a few men and dash toward the Tunstall store creating a diversion which would allow the others to run for the back gate from which they could escape to the river. By now there was no time for options. With their guns blazing, the Kid, Big Jim French, Jose Chaves y Chaves, Tom O'Folliard, and Harvey Morris darted through the doorway and raced toward the store. Morris was immediately felled by a slug. He died in his tracks. The others were met by gunfire coming from behind one corner of the Tunstall store. The Kid, and his group, changed directions and sprinted toward the river where they escaped to safety. Meanwhile, Robert Beckwith was in the wrong place at the wrong time. He had approached McSween's back door with a warrant urging him to surrender. Gunfire erupted again as McSween and the others attempted to run. Robert Beckwith was shot down, as was McSween who fell on top of him. Francisco Zamora and Vicente Romero made it to the chicken house before they also were killed. Yginio Salazar was gunned down near the rear gate, and left for dead. He would later crawl nearly a half mile to safety. Ignacio Gonzales was shot in the arm, but he reached the river and safety. Florencio Chaves and Jose Maria Sanchez escaped as well. Henry Brown, George Coe, and Sam Smith, who had been occupying the grain warehouse behind the Tunstall store, were also able to flee. The troops from Fort Stanton had done little more than to watch the confrontation, but their mere presence aided in the defeat of the McSween faction. The battle was over, but the war with Billy the Kid was not.

Following two more deaths in separate incidents, turmoil again mounted in Lincoln County. John Selman (who would later kill John Wesley Hardin—in the back) and his brother Tom joined forces with John Kinney, Jessie Evans, Jake Owens, and many other members of the old George Peppin posse. The gang was sometimes called "Selman's Scouts." On the 18th of August they raided the Feliz Ranch (the Tunstall ranch) and stole about two hundred head of cattle. The Regulators answered. Bonney, Bowdre, Scurlock, Middleton, and the others, were joined by ten new men, bringing their band to about thirty-six in number. On the 6th of September they rode to the Fritz Ranch (a Dolan-Riley stronghold) and proceeded to "rustle" one hundred and fifty head of cattle and fifteen horses.

President Rutherford B. Hayes gave all law breakers fair warning when he announced that beginning on the 13th of October the Army would again be permitted to furnish troops to support civil authorities. A marked decrease in lawlessness, and a semblance of civil order began to take place.

The Regulators began to break up. John Middleton, Henry Brown, Fred Waite, Frank and George Coe, and others abandoned their outlaw ways, at least for the time being, and departed in various directions to presumably earn an honest living. The others followed Billy the Kid.

A potentially dangerous parley occurred at Lincoln on February 18, 1879, ironically exactly one year after John Tunstall had been killed. Billy the Kid, Doc Scurlock, Tom O'Folliard, George Bowers, and Jose Salazar met with Jessie Evans, Jimmy Dolan, Billy Mathews, Billy Campbell, and Edgar Walz. Throwing this bunch together was like a powder keg waiting for someone to light the fuse. Incredibly, they agreed to a truce. Furthermore, they assented to aid each other in resisting arrests and never to give evidence against the other in any prosecution. Anyone who broke the pact was to be killed on sight. Following the parley, they all got drunk together. While heading down the street later that evening, the group encountered Houston Chapman, Susan McSween's lawyer. Billy Campbell (one of Dolan's men) shot, and killed Chapman at point blank range. Campbell proclaimed that he had "promised my God and General Dudley" that he would kill Chapman, and now he had done it. In the confusion that followed, the Kid and Tom O'Folliard slipped out of town, and headed for San Patricio.

Billy the Kid grew tired of running. He decided to write to the new territorial governor, Lew Wallace, in an effort to make a "deal." Bonney agreed to testify as a witness to the Chapman murder if Governor Wallace would grant him amnesty. Bonney further requested a meeting with the governor to discuss the matter. Governor Wallace (who was presently penning his classic novel *Ben Hur*) was intrigued by the idea and scheduled a secret meeting at the residence of old Squire Wilson the evening of March 15, 1879. The meeting materialized. The Kid walked in with a Winchester in one hand and a revolver in the other. The governor's plan was simple. Bonney would submit to arrest and would remain in jail until the Grand Jury convened. After he identified the murderers of Chapman, he would receive a pardon and be free to go. Bonney had good intentions and followed through with his part of the bargain. Wallace did not. District Attorney Rynerson saw to it that the Kid remained behind bars. Following the Grand Jury, the Kid waited twenty days for Wallace to come through before he took matters into his own hands. Billy the Kid and Tom O'Folliard (who had surrendered with him) easily escaped and headed toward Fort Sumner.

While drinking in Bob Hargrove's saloon at Fort Sumner, on January 10, 1880, the Kid was tipped off that a fellow standing by the bar named Joe Grant intended to kill him. Bonney, in his ever-smiling way, began admiring Grant's pearl-handled revolver. The Kid then innocently asked if he could examine it. While doing so, he noticed that there were only three cartridges in the cylinder, so before handing it back, he rotated the cylinder so that it would fire next on an empty chamber. Within a short while, Grant challenged the Kid. He thrust his six-gun toward Bonney's face and pulled the trigger. As the weapon clicked, the Kid fired a round into Grant's head. He died instantly. As with many of the Kid's episodes, this one has another version. Grant was also identified as being Texas Red, a bounty hunter intent on killing the Kid. In this version he faced Bonney, put his hand on his revolver, then stated, "Billy, I'll draw first blood for the drinks." Billy answered, "I'll go you," as he drew and killed the bounty hunter who was never able to clear leather. It is doubtful that Texas Red (or Grant) was hunting a bounty, for at this time Billy the Kid had no price on his head.

Surrounded by some of the original Regulators, the Kid went back to rustling cattle and horses. His gang took on a new look with the addition of many toughs like the scoundrel Dave Rudabaugh, Las Vegas killer John Webb, and Texas hard case Joe Cook. They thieved at will and nobody dared to stop them. Nobody, that is, until Pat Garrett came along.

Pat Garrett was a saloonkeeper and former buffalo hunter with nerves of steel. He was convinced to move from Fort Sumner to Lincoln and run for the office of sheriff. Garrett had strong support and was easily elected. The Kid was a frequent customer at Beaver Smith's Saloon where Garrett had worked, and they knew each other well. Garrett was determined to do well at his new position, which meant bringing in Billy the Kid, dead or alive. The new sheriff laid trap after trap, and came close, but continued to come up empty. On one occasion (December 19, 1880, near Fort Sumner), the Kid and Tom O'Folliard were riding ahead of the gang, trailed by Dave Rudabaugh, Billy Wilson, Charlie Bowdre, and Tom Pickett, when (whether by instinct or not) Billy wheeled his horse around and rode to the back of the pack to get some chewing tobacco from Billy Wilson. At that moment, Pat Garrett shouted, "Halt!" O'Folliard went for his gun, as the posse shot him down. The Kid and the others all escaped. O'Folliard died within the hour. Garrett and the posse turned their attention to tracking the Kid.

The Kid and his followers weren't able to disguise their trail through the snow. Four days later, at Stinking Springs, Garrett's posse cornered the fugitives in a dilapidated rock house that was once used as a forage station. The building had one door, and no windows or other openings. As it was about 2:00 a.m., Garrett decided to wait until daybreak. At dawn, Charlie Bowdre emerged from the building with a nosebag to feed his horse. Pat Garrett ordered him to throw up his hands, but Bowdre quickly drew two pistols and exchanged shots as three bullets crashed into his body. He staggered, then dropped dead. The others reached out and were able to pull two of the horses into the house. They intended to saddle them, then ride through the doorway with their six-shooters blazing. As they pulled the third horse, Garrett shot it down and it blocked the doorway

Thomas O'Folliard was unwavering in his allegiance to Billy the Kid. Conversely, Tom was Billy's closest friend. *Lincoln County Heritage Trust.*

making an escape virtually impossible. The Kid laughed and cracked jokes inside as if he hadn't a worry in the world. Later in the day the outlaws surrendered.

At La Mesilla, on April 13, 1881, Judge Warren H. Bristol pronounced sentence on William Bonney. He declared that the defendant shall be confined to prison in Lincoln County until May 13, 1881, at which time he shall "be hanged by the neck until his body be dead." As Bonney was chained in preparation for the one hundred and fifty mile journey to Lincoln, newspaper reporters indicated that the Kid looked quite cheerful.

Under heavy guard, Billy the Kid arrived back in Lincoln on April 21, 1881. He was incarcerated in the county courthouse (the old Murphy-Dolan store). The Kid was kept in leg and arm shackles, chained to the floor, and was guarded twenty-four hours a day. On the 28th of April, Deputy Robert Olinger led the other prisoners over to the Wortley Hotel for dinner. Deputy J. W. Bell remained at the courthouse to guard the Kid. While the others were away, Bonney told Bell that he needed to use the outhouse. Bell agreed to escort Billy outside, and he did. Upon their return to the courthouse, the Kid slipped his small hands out of the cuffs, produced a six-gun and shot Bell to death. Where the gun came from is a matter for speculation. Bonney could have grabbed Bell's revolver—then again, one may have been planted for him in the privy. Alerted as to the commotion, Robert Olinger left his prisoners in front of the hotel, and dashed across the street. As he neared the courthouse, Billy called out from an upstairs window, "Hello, Bob!" As Olinger looked up, the Kid blasted him with both barrels of a shotgun. Thirty-six buckshot entered his body. Billy the Kid then armed himself with two pistols and a Winchester, stepped out on to the porch, and in his usually jovial manner announced that he was "master not only of the courthouse, but also of the town." The Kid worked on his shackles for about an hour before he was able to free one leg. The town was paralyzed—nobody raised a finger to stop him. With a blanket roll, a few supplies, and an arsenal of weapons, Billy the Kid leisurely mounted a pony and rode out of town to the west. He stopped at Yginio Salazar's house where Yginio helped him remove the shackles, then furnished him a good horse. Though already famous, the escape from Lincoln made Billy the Kid legendary. Stories of his daring escapades rolled off the presses everywhere.

Under the circumstances, most fugitives would have traveled great distances to get as far away from Lincoln as possible. Not Billy the Kid, however, for he

The Lincoln County Courthouse (originally the Murphy-Dolan store) was the scene of Billy the Kid's most daring escape. *Lincoln County Heritage Trust.*

found a certain security amongst his circle of friends in the New Mexico Territory which he knew so well. In response to a rumor that the Kid was in the Fort Sumner area, Pat Garrett, Thomas McKinney, and John W. Poe headed in that direction. When they arrived, Garrett decided to stop by and see an old friend, Pete Maxwell, to inquire as to the whereabouts of the Kid. The sun had already set and Maxwell had retired early to his bedroom in the southeastern corner of the house. It was a warm evening on July 14, 1881, and Maxwell left his outside door wide open for circulation. While the others waited out front, Garrett stepped into the darkened bedroom to awaken Maxwell. Garrett sat on the edge of the bed as the two talked. Meanwhile, the Kid was staying at a nearby house. He had just returned from a rendezvous in a nearby peach orchard with Celsa Gutierrez, a Mexican girl that the Kid would occasionally "meet." Bonney was hungry, and he decided to cut a steak from a side of beef hanging in Pete Maxwell's smokehouse. The Kid spotted the men out front, and wondering who they were, went to the doorway and called out to Maxwell, "Pedro, quien sonos estos hombres

Three sheriffs of Lincoln County. Seated are Pat Garrett (at left) and John W. Poe. Standing between them is James Brent. *Wild Horse Collection.*

afuera?" Maxwell whispered to Garrett, "That's him!" Garrett drew his gun and fired, then leaped to the floor as he fired again. The second shot wasn't necessary as the first had hit its target right above the heart. Billy the Kid died instantly. He uttered no other word, nor did he know who killed him.

Jack Slade's Ravenswood Ranch above Meadow Creek in Madison County, Montana. *Montana Historical Society.*

JACK SLADE AND THE JULESBURG VENDETTA

In 1829, Joseph Alfred "Jack" Slade was born in Carlyle, Illinois, a community in which his father had been one of the town founders. Jack Slade joined the army at age 18 and headed west. He would become one of the most ornery characters on the western frontier.

The incidents which made Jack Slade legendary occurred during his tenure with the Overland Stage Company. Overland, it seems, had a ruthless and undependable stationmaster whom they desired to replace. Jules Beni ran the stage station at Julesburg, Colorado. The station was unprofitable as horses and supplies continued to disappear. Slade accepted the position and set out for Julesburg with Jule's discharge papers in his possession.

After his replacement by Slade, Beni remained in the area, and a deep resentment grew between the two. The animosity culminated at Julesburg, in 1858, when Jules Beni sought out Jack Slade and gunned him down. The former stationmaster emptied his pistol, then grabbed his shotgun and fired a blast into Slade's already wounded body. Certain that Slade was dying, Beni turned and departed.

Miraculously, Slade recovered. He had been hit by 13 slugs, several of which remained inside his body. Eventually he was strong enough to resume his duties as stationmaster.

Slade, who became known as Captain Jack, drove his workers hard to maximize efficiency. Coaches ran on schedule. The station at Julesburg became profitable for the Overland Stage Company. Jack Slade had gained a reputation for being a tough hombre—one who most certainly could defy death.

Following the shooting, Jules Beni fled the immediate area. But word filtered back to Jack that he was still in the territory, and furthermore, that he was boasting that he was going to finish Slade off once and for all. Captain Jack knew that he could not afford to have Jules catch him during another unsuspecting moment. So, Slade sent his men out to find the former stationmaster, with a bounty if they could capture him alive. Soon Slade received word that Beni had been captured at another relay station. Jack Slade saddled up and rode hard, with retaliation on his mind. When he arrived he found Jules tied to a corral fence post. According to legend, Slade shot Jules Beni several times in order to watch him die a slow death. Legend also has it that Slade sliced both ears off the corpse, then carried one around with him for many months.

As time passed, whiskey effected Jack Slade more and more. When drunk he would become reckless and obnoxious. His circle of friends remained loyal to him regardless of the circumstances. His wife, Virginia, stood by him through thick and thin. Numerous stories of shootings, beatings, stabbings and hangings are attributed to Jack Slade. He had become a menace to society.

Overland transferred Slade across the territory to a new stage station which he named Virginia Dale in honor of his wife. Slade's reputation followed him, and the violence continued. Eventually he became so intolerable to the Overland Stage Company that they fired him. Shortly thereafter Slade was involved in a shooting in Wyoming. When a warrant was issued for his arrest, Jack and Virginia fled to the gold fields of Montana.

Rich placer gold had just been discovered at Alder Gulch, and Virginia City was a booming new mining town when the Slades arrived in 1863. Rather than chase the mother lode, however, Captain Jack decided to establish a freighting business. Slade borrowed heavily to set up his new enterprise, and although it looked like he was making a substantial amount of money, he was deeply in debt. When he was sober, Jack Slade was a benevolent and charming individual. He attracted a new group of friends who seemed to follow him, even through his frequent spells of intoxication.

The Montana gold camps were virtually lawless, largely because of the infamous sheriff Henry Plummer. Plummer ran his operation from Skinner's Saloon in nearby Bannack. Although it was unknown to the citizens of Bannack, he was the leader of a large band of outlaws. Plummer knew when gold shipments departed, and upon which stagecoaches payrolls were due. A tip to his gang was usually followed by a robbery or hijacking. Business owners and gold miners finally had their fill of ineffective law enforcement and took matters into their own hands. On December 23, 1863, a band of vigilantes was organized. The assemblage was large, heavily armed, and would be effective. Jack Slade's freight wagons had been a target of Plummer's band, so he joined the vigilantes.

When the vigilantes captured gang member Red Yeager in early January, he confessed to several crimes and informed the group that Henry Plummer was his leader. Hopeful of saving his own neck, Yeager passed along the names of each of his cohorts. It was all the vigilantes would need. Yeager was hanged anyway. By February 3, 1864, eighteen other members of the gang, including Henry Plummer, had been hanged or shot to death. The vigilantes with whom Jack Slade rode would soon bring about his own demise.

It wasn't unusual for drunks to raise a ruckus in a booming gold camp. When the ruckus resulted in destruction of property and beatings and insults of innocent citizens, it was a detriment to society. Such was the case with Jack Slade. He and his friends would gallop down the street firing their six-shooters into the air, or would ride their horses into a store or saloon intent upon destroying supplies within. Jack Slade had become a major detriment to the community. When sober Slade would pay restitution for his dastardly deeds, but warning after warning regarding his conduct went unheeded.

The Vigilance Committee, realizing that enough was enough, ruled that Slade should die. On March 10, 1864, a weeping and begging Jack Slade was hanged from a beam supported by two gate posts just outside Virginia City. When word reached Virginia Slade as to what was happening, she rode into town at breakneck speed. She was too late. The body had already been moved to the Virginia Hotel, where it was laid out. The shrill cries of Virginia Slade attested to her love for Jack.

William Mitchell was determined to attain revenge. *Hood County Museum*

THE MITCHELL-TRUITT AFFAIR

Bill Mitchell was the personification of a tough Texas cowboy. He was a crack marksman and a master with a rope. His leather-beaten face and fine horsemanship were the result of much time spent in the saddle. Bill Mitchell was as imposing an individual as there was in Hood County. He would also become the central figure in the bloody Mitchell-Truitt feud.

William Nelson Mitchell was the seventh child of Nelson "Cooney" Mitchell and his wife Nancy. Bill was born April 16, 1852. Following the Civil War, the Mitchell clan (which consisted of Bill, his parents, two of his brothers and two of his sisters) established a ranch along the Brazos River at a place that would become known as Mitchell's Bend. One day while Bill and Cooney were out rounding up strays they stumbled upon a large family of poor and destitute squatters. It was obvious to the Mitchells that the Truitt family was underfed and needed help. Needing additional hands on his growing ranch, Cooney Mitchell made the Truitts an offer they couldn't refuse. He would help them build a log home and smokehouse and provide them food until they became self-sufficient. In turn, the Truitts would work for the Mitchells. Part of the Truitt's compensation would pay off their indebtedness to the Mitchells.

Eventually, the Truitts were able to get along without any help. They paid off their debt to the Mitchells (the Truitts at least thought so) and became independent. It wasn't long before they had purchased a piece of property adjacent to Mitchell land. It would be the catalyst for much trouble.

Along the property line where the Truitt land adjoined that of the Mitchells there was a strip which both families claimed to own. Their argument finally wound up in court during March of 1874. The courtroom battle was heated as tempers flew on both sides. The trial (which was ultimately won by the Truitts) aroused a hatred which would quickly turn to violence.

The Truitt boys left the courthouse and had traveled about six miles on their way home when they were confronted by Bill Mitchell, his father, two brother-in-laws and a neighbor. Evidently, the younger Truitts jeered the Mitchells over the

James Morgan Truitt was a minister and newspaperman when he met his demise. *Hood County Museum*

outcome of the trial. This action further incensed the Mitchells who opened fire on the Truitts. Sam and Ike Truitt were killed instantly. Jim, the eldest Truitt (who was a minister), was able to take refuge at a nearby house after he was wounded. A few days later Cooney Mitchell, his son-in-law W. J. Owens and their neighbor James Shaw were arrested and charged with murder. Bill Mitchell and his brother-in-law Mitch Graves were able to elude the law and became fugitives.

During the ensuing trial, the Reverend Jim Truitt testified against the Mitchells. The jury was convinced that he told the truth. Cooney Mitchell was sentenced to be executed by hanging. Owens and Shaw were also convicted and sentenced to the penitentiary.

One night, while Cooney Mitchell awaited execution, a heavily armed individual attempted to approach the rear of the jailhouse. A guard shot the shadowy figure who toppled down an embankment toward the river. The next morning the body of Jeff Mitchell, Cooney's youngest son, was found. He had been shot through the head.

A crowd gathered for Cooney Mitchell's execution. Before the noose was placed around his neck, Mitchell was asked if he had any last words. Cooney Mitchell called out to his son Bill, wherever he might be, to avenge his father's death. This onus probably didn't make any difference. Bill Mitchell was the kind of individual who would seek revenge anyway.

After the death of Cooney Mitchell the rest of his family left Mitchell's Bend. The Truitts moved on shortly thereafter. Over ten years would pass before Bill Mitchell and Jim Truitt would meet again.

Truitt moved from parish to parish throughout eastern Texas, until he finally wound up at Timpson. There he supplemented his ministry by operating the local newspaper.

Bill Mitchell also moved about during this period. Using the alias of John W. King, Mitchell lived in Fort Stanton, New Mexico, where he worked as a teamster. Although he was not involved in the Lincoln County War, he was there during its worst days. Mitchell returned to Texas and assumed a new alias, John Davis, the name he used when he married Mary Beckett. They lived together, with Mary's father, in an isolated area west of San Antonio. The couple had one child, Maud Jane.

On July 20, 1886, Bill Mitchell rode into Timpson. After receiving directions to the Truitt residence, he walked through the door without knocking. To the horror of Julia Truitt, Jim's wife, and their daughter, Bill Mitchell drew his revolver and shot Jim Truitt through the head. The fugitive then walked outside, mounted his horse and rode away.

It was two full days before Sheriff A. J. Spradley, from Nacogdoches, was summoned and could hit the trail in pursuit of Mitchell. Spradley was not able to track Mitchell very far, so he returned to Timpson.

Twenty-one years passed before Sheriff Swofford of Hood County received a tip that Bill Mitchell was back in Lincoln County, New Mexico, living under his newest alias, Baldy Russell. Swofford and a deputy traveled to New Mexico and located Mitchell. Posing as cattlemen, the lawmen gained his confidence. When the opportunity arose, and Mitchell's guard was down, the lawmen jumped on their prey and handcuffed him. Mitchell was returned to Hood County, Texas, to stand trial for the murders of Ike and Sam Truitt in 1874. An old piece of evidence surfaced which had not been used at Cooney Mitchell's trial. A derringer which belonged to young Ike had one empty chamber. The Mitchells had maintained all along that Ike Truitt fired the first shot. The jury agreed that this was possible, and acquitted Bill Mitchell.

Bill Mitchell was also indicted in the death of Jim Truitt. Mrs. Julia Truitt Bishop, who had remarried and by now was an accomplished writer, traveled from Chicago to identify Bill Mitchell as her ex-husband's murderer. Following a hung jury, the accused was released under a $20,000 bond. Following another hung jury the venue was changed to Cherokee County and once again Bill Mitchell posted bond. He journeyed back to New Mexico from where he furnished sworn affidavits that he was unable to travel to Texas due to illness. His case was continued several times before he finally appeared in court on December 23, 1910. This time he was found guilty, a decision which was upheld two years later by the Court of Criminal Appeals. At the age of sixty-four Bill Mitchell was sent to prison.

After serving just two years of his sentence, Bill Mitchell escaped. Using the alias of John Davis once again, Mitchell eventually settled down in Arizona. At a hospital in San Simon, with Mary at his side, Bill Mitchell died of heart failure on June 26, 1928. He was 76 years old.

The Tewksbury homestead (photographed shortly after the Pleasant Valley War). John Tewksbury and William Jacobs were shot to death at this location on September 2, 1887. *Arizona Historical Society*.

THE PLEASANT VALLEY WAR

In the Tonto Basin of Arizona lie the lush pastures of Pleasant Valley, scene of the bloody Graham-Tewksbury feud. The conflict between the Grahams (a clan of Iowa natives) and the Tewksburys (who were partially of Indian blood) had its roots in cattle, but was nurtured by greed, prejudice, hatred and revenge. Some historians have indicated that the Graham-Tewksbury feud was a battle between cattlemen and sheepmen. That is only partially true. Violence was initiated (in February 1887) in an incident between range riders and sheepherders, but the trouble had started much earlier. Basically, the feud began as a conflict between cattle rustlers. It was a game of who could get away with the most. They stole cattle and they stole horses, usually under the cover of darkness. They would hide the stock until the new brands healed, at which time the animals were driven to market in Mexico and elsewhere. The rustlers were predominately a clique of friends who rode for area ranches. Cherry Creek loosely became a dividing line. Thieves from the west of Cherry Creek stole from ranches to the east, and vice-versa. As hostilities heated up, the factions became more defined, and territorial guidelines more evident. For the most part, the territory west of Cherry Creek belonged to the Graham faction, while that to the east became Tewksbury country.

Roughly a mile and a half separated the Graham and Tewksbury ranches.

At one time the two families got along fine. In fact, they were partners in a rustling operation. They would pick up strays belonging to other ranchers, divide the stock, and apply their own brands. Evidently, the bitterness precipitated in 1883 following an incident in which the Grahams allegedly branded some stolen stock without advising the Tewksburys. There were many factors, however, that led to the heightening of animosities.

The Blevins clan would become an integral part of the feud. Mart Blevins, and four of his sons (John, Charles, Hampton and Sam), established a small ranch near the headwaters of Canyon Creek in 1884. The Blevins would align with the Grahams. When Andy, the fifth son, arrived in Pleasant Valley, the Grahams gained an unscrupulous ally. Andy Blevins, who used the alias Andy Cooper, was wanted by the law in both Texas and Oklahoma. Some of Andy's friends (also of questionable character) hired on with the huge Hash Knife outfit. Several Hash Knife cowboys became players in the Graham-Tewksbury feud.

The Hash Knife outfit (officially the Aztec Land and Cattle Company) owned a massive tract of land above the Mogollon Rim, north of Pleasant Valley. Their estimated 60,000 head of cattle often grazed in the Tonto Basin. The Hash Knife outfit never became directly involved in the Pleasant Valley War, but some of their cowboys did. John Paine was an excessive drinker who was always ready for a fight. Tom Tucker (who later would become a lawman) seemed to have a nose for trouble. Tom Pickett was accustomed to danger, having ridden with Billy the Kid in the Lincoln County War. Other Hash Knife toughs became involved in Pleasant Valley "activities" as well.

During late 1885, 1886, and much of 1887, rustling in Arizona Territory had reached enormous proportions. Stolen stock from southern Arizona would be driven north to the canyons around Tonto Basin. Brands were "doctored" before the animals were taken to various northern markets. On their return trip, the rustlers would gather a new herd and drive them to Tonto Basin before they were eventually moved on to market places further south. The stock was usually horses for they could be moved rapidly.

Many people believed that Andy Cooper, the Blevins family, Paine, Tucker and Pickett were the heart of the rustling operation. Because they were identifiable friends of the Graham family, the Grahams also became the object of accusations. And so it was, when the Tewksburys had horses stolen, they immediately pointed their fingers at the Grahams. Though no evidence indicated they were involved in the horse stealing ring, the Grahams were implicated for two reasons. They had done some rustling of their own in the past, and they associated with known horse thieves.

The Daggs brothers (of Flagstaff) owned a large herd of sheep which had grazed on open land north of the Mogollon Rim prior to its purchase as a part of extensive acreage acquired by the Hash Knife outfit. The Hash Knife was intent upon driving sheepherders from their vast new holdings. In February 1887, P.P. Daggs ordered his sheepherders to move the flock south, over the Mogollon Rim, and into Pleasant Valley. As the sheepherders neared the pass which led over the Mogollon Rim they were ambushed. One of Dagg's herders (a Basque from Spain) was shot to death and then beheaded. Many of the sheep were driven over a sheer cliff to their death. William Jacobs and two fellow sheepherders, both Indian, moved the remaining sheep down to the Tewksbury ranch where they sought refuge. In much the same manner that the Grahams were drawn into the worsening hostilities, so now were the Tewksburys.

Five months later, Mart Blevins (father of the five brothers) rode out to retrieve some strays that had wandered from their grazing area. He never returned. The Blevins and their Hash Knife friends made an exhausting search for the old man, but to no avail. Their assumption was that he had been killed. Naturally, they accused the Tewksburys.

On the 9th of August, a confrontation occurred at the Newton ranch. Jim Tewksbury, Ed Tewksbury, Jim Roberts and Joseph Boyer were inside Newton's cabin when Hampton Blevins, John Paine, Tom Tucker, Bob Gillespie and Bob Carrington rode up to the front door. Paine asked Jim Tewksbury (who had stepped to the front door) if they could come in. Tewksbury advised him that Newton's cabin wasn't a boarding house. There are conflicting reports as to who fired the first shot, but suddenly gunfire erupted in both directions. Slugs hit Hampton Blevins and John Paine. Both toppled dead from their horses. One shot hit Tucker in the chest, another nicked one of his ears. He managed to spur his mount and get away. Gillespie and Carrington each received superficial wounds. They whirled their horses and scampered away in another direction. None of the four gunmen inside the cabin were hurt. The carcasses of two horses laid beside the bodies of Blevins and Paine. When Tucker wasn't seen for two days, Bob Gillespie rode out and found him. Having lost much blood, Tucker had been too weak to return home on his own. He had struggled to the cabin of Bob Sigsby where he had taken refuge. Tom Tucker would later recover.

James D. Houck was a newly appointed deputy sheriff of Apache County (where Commodore Perry Owens was sheriff). Houck was also a brother-in-law of the Basque sheepherder who was slain and decapitated near the pass over Mogollon Rim. He was, therefore, sympathetic to the Tewksbury cause. On the evening of August 17, 1887, Jim Houck (who was carrying a warrant for the arrest of John Graham) encountered eighteen-year-old Billy Graham who was returning home from a dance. At the sight of each other, both men drew and fired several rounds. Graham was wounded. He booted his mount and raced toward home. Billy Graham died two days later.

By now, the battle was full-blown. There were no lawmen in Tonto Basin, and none arrived until the first of September. Sheriff William Mulvenon (of Yavapai County) and a small posse rode in, surveyed the situation, and then departed without making any arrests.

A story, which cannot be substantiated, claimed that the Grahams offered a bounty for the death of any Tewksbury. One evening a sniper was spotted by Jim and Ed Tewksbury. Jim fired a volley which seriously wounded the attacker, who was left to bleed to death.

Faced with increasing danger, John Blevins relocated with his wife, mother, and youngest brother to the town of Holbrook (about 75 miles away). Andy Cooper and his brother, Charles Blevins, remained in Pleasant Valley.

At dawn, on September 2, 1887, Andy Cooper and several cohorts waited in seclusion outside the Tewksbury cabin. John Tewksbury and William Jacobs emerged from within and began to gather up some horses. A barrage of gunfire dropped the two in their tracks. They were both killed instantly. The gunmen held the cabin in siege throughout the day, as hogs (it is said) chewed on the bodies of Tewksbury and Jacobs. After nightfall, those who had been pinned down in the cabin were able to slip away under the cover of darkness. The following day, Andy Cooper set out for the Blevins' house at Holbrook in order to lie low for awhile.

Sheriff Commodore Perry Owens rode (from Navajo Springs) to Holbrook, on the morning of September 4, 1887, in order to question the Blevins women as to the whereabouts of Andy Cooper. Anticipating no trouble, Owens rode alone. When he arrived at the house in Holbrook, he tied up his horse, then routinely withdrew one of his Winchesters which he carried as he approached the porch.

Suddenly Owens spotted Andy Cooper, with pistol in hand, peering from the front door. Both men fired simultaneously. Cooper dropped where he stood —dead. John Blevins also fired at the sheriff from the front door. Owens shot Blevins through the right shoulder and he went down as well. The sheriff looked for cover and dashed around the side of the house. As he did, he spotted Mose Roberts, (an in-law) who had emerged from the rear of the house with his

Commodore Perry Owens, sheriff of Apache County, Arizona, was a deadly marksman. *Arizona Historical Society.*

six-shooter in hand. Owens' rifle barked again, and Roberts fell dead. As Sam Houston Blevins (youngest of the brothers) ran onto the front porch brandishing his revolver, Perry Owens shot him through the heart. The deadly sheriff had killed three men and wounded another in rapid succession. John Blevins was taken into custody and jailed at St. Johns.

Upon the suggestion of Governor C. Meyer Zulick, Sheriff William Mulvenon raised a large posse—one which was capable of fighting both the Grahams and Tewksburys if necessary in order to end the Pleasant Valley War. On the 9th of September, Mulvenon left Prescott and headed to Payson where he met Deputy Sheriff John W. Francis who had arrived from Flagstaff with several lawmen. Also joining the posse were Jim Houck (the deputy sheriff who shot Billy Graham) and George Newton—both Tewksbury partisans. Houck and Newton were influential in convincing Mulvenon to round up the Grahams first.

Perkin's store (a stone building once used for protection against Apaches) was located near both the Graham ranch and the cabin of Al Rose (a Graham supporter). Shortly before dawn on the 21st of September, the posse took occupancy of the store and an unfinished stone building nearby. While most of the lawmen remained behind the walls, six others rode around the vicinity. Mulvenon's ploy was intended to draw some of the Graham men out to investigate who the strangers were. The decoy partially worked. John Graham and Charles Blevins cautiously rode toward Perkin's store, circled it, then rode over to the unfinished building. Mulvenon sprang from hiding and ordered the two to raise their hands. Graham and Blevins whirled their horses and drew their guns. It

Thomas Graham, a principal figure in the Pleasant Valley War, was killed in 1892. *Arizona Historical Society.*

was a mistake. Both men were blown from their saddles by a barrage of lead from the posse's weapons. Blevins died instantly. The posse left John Graham to die and headed toward the Graham ranch in hopes of arresting his brother Tom. At Graham's place Mulvenon found badly injured Joe Underwood, his wife, their two small children, and Miguel Apocada, a Mexican hand. Apocada was arrested. Tom Graham had managed to elude the trap. Shortly thereafter, the posse rode to Al Rose's cabin. Rose gave up without a fight.

George Newton left the posse a day earlier and rode to the Tewksbury ranch. He convinced Mulvenon that the Tewksbury clan would surrender peacefully. When the posse arrived Newton was waiting with six others. Ed and Jim Tewksbury, Jim Roberts, George Wagner, Jake Lauffer and Joe Boyer turned themselves in, as did George Newton. With their nine prisoners the posse left for Prescott.

As the cast of characters died, so did the Graham-Tewksbury feud. Jim Tewksbury died (in 1888) from tuberculosis. Cool-headed Thomas Graham was murdered in 1892 virtually ending the Pleasant Valley War. Ed Tewksbury was tried for Graham's murder, but was acquitted. He would later become a lawman at Globe, Arizona.

Wyatt Earp, whose character was questionnable, had nerves of steel and a cold heart when discharging his duties. *Denver Public Library, Western History Department.*

THE EARP-CLANTON VENDETTA

It has been suggested that Wyatt Earp and the Clantons were cohorts in some cattle rustling escapades, and that their dislike for each other originated then. There seems to be no proof to substantiate this theory, but it is a possibility. Before his Tombstone, Arizona days, Wyatt Earp was in and out of trouble. He was arrested for horse stealing, arrested for fighting, reprimanded for neglecting to turn in fines he had collected from prostitutes while a policeman in Wichita, and was run out of Las Vegas, New Mexico for attempting to work a swindle with "Mysterious" Dave Mather. Wyatt, Morgan, and Virgil Earp had been feuding for some time with Ike and Billy Clanton and Frank and Tom McLaury, all known rustlers.

Certainly, there was bitterness when Tom and Frank McLaury testified against Wyatt's friend Doc Holliday in connection with the attempted stagecoach robbery at Drew's Station during which two men were killed. Holliday was acquitted, but the McLaurys had earned his resentment.

There were other factors which led to the distaste each faction had for the other. Mrs. Virgil Earp indicated that the Earp family was outraged following a late-night rendezvous between James Earp's sixteen-year-old stepdaughter, Hattie Earp, and one of the McLaury brothers. It is also possible that some of the animosity could be traced to a gambling quarrel.

Virgil Earp was city marshal of Tombstone. John Behan was sheriff of Cochise County. Their offices (both located in Tombstone) didn't agree on much, including law enforcement. Behan was a friend of the hard-drinking Clanton clan and therefore was considered a nuisance by Virgil Earp and his brothers. As the dispute between the Earps and Clantons intensified, Virgil swore Morgan and Wyatt in as his deputies.

Virgil Earp was city marshal of Tombstone during the gunfight at the O.K. Corral. *Kansas State Historical Society.*

On October 25, 1881, Ike Clanton and Tom McLaury arrived at Tombstone in a wagon to pick up supplies. That night and the following morning Doc Holliday taunted Ike Clanton, attempting to bully him into a fight. Wyatt, Morgan and Virgil Earp added to the belittling. On the morning of the 26th, Wyatt approached Tom McLaury, drew his revolver, and challenged him to fight. When McLaury refused, Wyatt hit him with his gun barrel. Before noon Billy Clanton and Frank McLaury rode into town. When Frank McLaury left his mount on the boardwalk and entered a store, Wyatt grabbed his horse by the bit. Frank emerged from the store and the two had heated words. "Keep him off the sidewalk," demanded Earp who further stated, "It's against the city ordinance." A short time later Billy Claiborne, a Clanton rider, arrived in town. As things began to boil, Sheriff John Behan approached both factions in a futile attempt to get them to lay down their arms. Ike Clanton and Tom McLaury indicated that they were unarmed. Tom McLaury further advised that he had given his gun and gun belt to Andy Mehan, a local saloonkeeper, for safe keeping—and that he wanted no further trouble.

At approximately 2:00 p.m., Doc Holliday (who had just been deputized), Wyatt, Morgan and Virgil Earp approached the Clantons, McLaurys, and Billy Claiborne. Doc Holliday had a shotgun and carried a six gun in his belt. Wyatt, Morgan and Virgil Earp carried six-shooters. Billy Clanton, Billy Claiborne, and Frank McLaury were also armed with revolvers. Tom McLaury and Ike Clanton were unarmed. The Earps and Holliday confronted the others at the edge of a narrow lot on Fremont Street (near the O.K. Corral) between Fly's Gallery (a photography studio) and the Harwood house. Wyatt barked, "You've been looking for a fight and now you can have it!" As somewhat of a contradiction, Virgil snapped, "Throw up your hands!" The shooting commenced. Morgan actually got off the first shot hitting Billy Clanton in the right wrist. Wyatt fired and shot Frank McLaury in the stomach. Ike Clanton and Billy Claiborne ran. Claiborne ducked into the rear door of the photography studio and disappeared. Tom McLaury had been standing behind his horse. When the first shots rang out, the horse shied and Doc Holliday cut Tom McLaury down with his shotgun. Twelve buckshot had penetrated a four-inch area on his right side. Although wounded, Billy Clanton had drawn with his left hand and a bullet from his gun hit Virgil Earp in the leg. Holliday tossed away his shotgun and drew his pistol. Somehow the badly wounded Frank McLaury also drew. Several bullets flew in each direction. McLaury shot Holliday in the hip before taking a bullet in the neck—probably from Morgan Earp, but possibly from Holliday. Another slug from Billy Clanton's gun hit Morgan Earp in the shoulder, but Morgan continued to fire and either he or Wyatt finished off Billy Clanton. The shooting stopped.

Tom McLaury, Frank McLaury, and Billy Clanton were dead. Morgan Earp,

Virgil Earp, and Doc Holliday were wounded. There has been much discussion as to who were the bad guys and who were the good guys in this encounter—and there will continue to be. The Earp bunch was stripped of their badges, and accused of murder, but their actions were eventually deemed "justified." Nothing was resolved. The gunfight at the O.K. Corral was but one chapter in the Earp-Clanton feud.

John Henry "Doc" Holliday, the gunfighting and gambling dentist, was a close friend of Wyatt Earp. *Kansas State Historical Society.*

Though the Earps and Doc Holliday felt justice had been served at the O.K. Corral, Clanton sympathizers felt otherwise. They carried heavy grudges toward the Earps.

The first incident of retaliation occurred December 28, 1881, at approximately 11:30 p.m.. Tombstone was in a fairly festive holiday mood. Virgil Earp exited the Oriental Saloon and stepped out into the street. As he did so, shotgun blasts pierced the night. Virgil fell to the ground. He was quickly carried into a nearby hotel, and a doctor went to work on him. Most of the buckshot wounds were in his left arm, which was badly torn. More buckshot had penetrated his left side and back. Virgil told Wyatt, who had hastened to his side, "When they get me under, don't let them take my arm off. If I have to be buried, I want both arms on me." His arm was saved.

On the evening of March 18, 1882 at Campbell and Hatch's Billiard Parlor on Allen Street, Tombstone, Morgan Earp was enjoying a game of billiards with Bob Hatch. There were several onlookers, including Wyatt Earp. At 10:50 p.m., Morgan reached for the chalk to chalk his cue as shots rang out from the rear door of the billiard hall. One bullet sped through Morgan's stomach, shattered his spinal column, passed through his body and superficially wounded George Berry, a bystander. Another bullet barely missed Wyatt. Morgan stated, "This is the last game of pool I'll ever play." With Wyatt, Virgil, Warren, James, and the Earp women at his side, Morgan died within the hour. The revenge killing was generally thought to have been performed by Clanton supporters Frank Stilwell, Pete Spence, Florentino Cruz, and possibly others. The Earps were sure that they had done it.

Following Morgan's death, it was agreed that Virgil and his wife should leave Tombstone. He was still injured and would be easy prey for another attack. On March 20, 1882, Mr. and Mrs. Virgil Earp were escorted to Tucson by Wyatt Earp, Warren Earp, Doc Holliday, Sherman McMasters and "Turkey Creek" Jack Johnson. There was a reason for all the protection. They had heard that Frank Stilwell and Ike Clanton were in Tucson. The group arrived at the railroad depot, and following a search of the train to California, the Virgil Earps boarded.

Frank Stilwell was spotted near the depot. Wyatt gave chase, with the others close behind. They quickly tracked him down and at close range the group opened fire. Stilwell's lifeless body slumped to the ground. He was riddled with holes and had a bad powder burn on one hand as if he had grabbed a shotgun barrel.

After returning to Tombstone the Earp party set out in search of other members of the Clanton bunch. Late morning, on March 22, 1882, they rode to Pete Spence's place. They were unaware that Spence was sitting in the Tombstone jail along with Indian Charley, a gambler named Freis, and other suspects in the death of Morgan Earp. But at Spence's wood camp, the group found another suspect in Morgan Earp's murder—Florentino Cruz. The same group, Wyatt and Warren Earp, Holliday, McMasters, and Johnson riddled Cruz with bullets much the same way they had Stilwell two days earlier.

Shortly thereafter the rest of the Earp group left the Tombstone area. There was no further retaliation by either faction. The gunfight at the O.K. Corral and the Earp-Clanton feud stand in the forefront of confrontations in the Old West.

Morgan Earp was shot to death on March 18, 1882 while playing pool at Campbell and Hatch's Billiard Parlor in Tombstone. *Kansas State Historical Society.*

Gunfire trapped Jim Masterson in the temporary courthouse at Cimarron. *Wild Horse Collection.*

BATTLE FOR THE GRAY COUNTY SEAT

Two noted gunmen, former city marshals of Dodge City, Jim Masterson and Bill Tilghman were involved in the famous "Battle for the Gray County Seat" at Cimarron, Kansas. Factions from the towns of Ingalls and Cimarron had been squabbling for some time for the right to be county seat. Cimarron, eighteen miles west of Dodge City, had a population of about 1,500. Ingalls, with a population of only two hundred, was situated six miles west of Cimarron. Although smaller, Ingalls was supported by multimillionaire Asa T. Soule, who had made his fortune from a concoction called "Hop Bitters." Soule wanted Ingalls to be the county seat and he freely spent much money toward this goal. He promised the residents of Montezuma and Hess a railroad from Dodge City if they would vote solidly for Ingalls as county seat. Soule also promised a sugar mill to the township of Ensign. Cimarron also attempted to "buy" votes by offering the township of Foote $10,000 which they backed with a bond. It was later determined that the bond was a forgery, and the township received nothing. The election was held on Monday, October 31, 1887, amid accusations on both sides of ballot box stuffing and other fraudulent activities. Ingalls won by a majority of 236 votes. The county records were moved to Ingalls on February 21, 1888. When A .T. Riley of Cimarron was appointed County Clerk pro tem, the records were returned to Cimarron where they were housed at the temporary courthouse, located on the second floor of the building at 115 S. Main Street.

When new elections were held for the county clerk's office in November of 1888, an Ingalls man, Newt F. Watson, defeated the clerk from Cimarron. When he demanded that the county records be moved to Ingalls, the protest came to a boil. When the town of Cimarron refused to relinquish the county records, Ingalls (and Asa Soule) decided to take them by force. They organized a raiding party which included several Dodge City gunmen.

Among them was Jim Masterson who was a more active gunfighter than his brother Bat. Years later, Dodge City resident George Bolds (a former Gray County official) reflected on Jim Masterson: "I can still shut my eyes and see him walking down the street, six-shooter under his coat, hat tilted to one side, a cigar in the corner of his mouth and his face as impassive as an Indian's. I maintain he was the most deadly man with a gun outside Harvey Logan, the executioner for the Wild Bunch in Wyoming. If Jim Masterson had ever met Logan or that buck-toothed Billy the Kid, my chips would have been on Jim." Bill Tilghman was also a highly respected gunman. As marshal he served Dodge City well, behind a unique badge made from two twenty-dollar gold pieces. He would later become a state senator in Oklahoma. Among the other hired guns from Dodge City were Fred Singer, Neil Brown, and Ben Daniels.

Newly elected Sheriff J .H. Reynolds (an Ingalls man) did not participate with the raiding party because he was recuperating from wounds received during a chase of rustlers. Newt Watson was accompanied by the gunmen and others including the aforementioned George Bolds. The raiding party, all of whom were deputized, numbered ten.

The raid occurred Saturday, January 12, 1889. At approximately 11:30 a.m., the Ingalls group arrived by wagon at the temporary courthouse in Cimarron. A few of the men ascended the stairs where they found A. T. Riley at work. At gunpoint, they demanded the county records. Riley had no choice but to oblige them. Word of the raid spread quickly around Cimarron. No sooner had the county books been loaded into a wagon, when Cimarron townspeople opened fire on the group near the wagon. The Ingalls men returned their fire as they somehow managed to climb into the wagon. With Charlie Reicheldeffer at the reins, and the county records in their possession, they dashed out of town leaving four of their cohorts trapped on the second floor of the courthouse. Four members of the Ingall's faction were wounded as bullets flew in both directions. Tilghman was nicked in the leg. Bolds took two slugs—one in the head, another in the leg. Ed Brooks and Charlie Reicheldeffer also suffered severe injuries.

Drew and Will Evans fought for the Cimarron faction during the battle for the Gray County seat. *City of Cimarron.*

In addition to the previously mentioned casualties to the Ingalls faction, one of the Cimarron men, J. W. English, had taken a slug in the head, and was dead. Ed Fairhurst and Jack Bliss received serious injuries, and a fellow named Harrington had a superficial wound. Altogether there were eight casualties—one dead and seven wounded.

Masterson and the others returned the fire from the second floor windows. A few members of the Cimarron group worked their way into the lower story of the courthouse, and fired shots up through the floor at the remaining Ingalls men. Trapped were Jim Masterson, Fred Singer, Billy Allensworth, and Newt Watson.

They climbed on top of desks, filing cabinets, and a safe to avoid being hit. The siege lasted for six hours.

After receiving a telegram from the mayor of Cimarron, Sheriff Reynolds pulled his injured body out of bed and rode into Cimarron in order to escort the men back to Ingalls and safety.

A story is told that the Cimarron forces agreed to end the siege following the receipt of a telegram from Bat Masterson. Supposedly, he informed them that if his brother and the others were not allowed to leave town, he would "come in with enough men to blow Cimarron off the face of Kansas." There seems to be no truth to this story.

At any rate, the county records remained at Ingalls until Cimarron won them back in the election of February 1893, at which time they were returned to Cimarron for good. Today, Cimarron remains the county seat of Gray County.

Volney Gibson, a Jaybird, was one of the central figures in the political feud at Richmond. *Fort Bend Museum.*

THE JAYBIRD-WOODPECKER FEUD

Richmond, Texas, was the scene of a political rivalry that ultimately turned into a blood bath. In the late 1880s the population of Fort Bend County was nearly eighty percent Black. The reins of political power were controlled by the Woodpeckers, who consisted of carpetbaggers, local Republicans (who wouldn't admit to being Republicans), and a few prominent Blacks, all of which were controlled by the Black vote. Jaybirds, on the other hand, consisted of the majority of the Caucasian population—that which one would consider to be "Southern white." Jaybirds accused Woodpeckers of much graft, which included assessing taxes based on one's political views. Much hatred grew between the two factions. The division was political, racial and social.

How the two groups got their strange names is a matter of speculation. County administrators were sometimes called Peckerwoods, which probably evolved into Woodpeckers as the term Jaybirds became popular. Presumably, the upstart Jaybirds received their title from the Blacks because they were "uppity like a jaybird." On July 2, 1888, the Jaybirds officially launched the Young Men's Democratic Club of Fort Bend County. The club was organized "to secure a wise, impartial, economical and unselfish administration of the affairs of our county"; and furthermore to terminate the rule by "the arbitrary and selfish minority that has so long disregarded the consent of the governed." They were fighting words. The battle lines had been set.

The leader of the Jaybirds was H. H. Frost, a merchant who operated the Brahma Bull and Red Hot Bar, a general store and saloon. He was aggressive, vivacious and had guts which helped earn him the nickname "Red Hot" Frost. Though a saloonkeeper, Frost had a little religion. Carry Nation (later to gain fame as a temperance advocate), who conducted a Sunday school class, once said of him, "One poor saloonkeeper named Frost came several times and always gave a dollar." The forces behind the Woodpeckers were James Wesson Parker, a member of the State Legislature, Sheriff Jim Garvey, and Jake Blakely, a former sheriff.

Judge J. W. Parker was a driving force behind the Woodpeckers. *George Memorial Library.*

Justice of the Peace, J. H. Shamblin, an active Jaybird, was shot to death at his home on the 2nd of August. The murder was committed by William Caldwell, a Black who was facing trial in Shamblin's court for cotton theft. Caldwell was tried, found guilty, and was executed by hanging. Although Shamblin's murderer seemingly had no political roots, Jaybirds blamed Woodpeckers for the incident.

Several minor altercations intensified the brewing feud. On August 16, 1888, a barbecue was held in Pittsville at which several Jaybirds and Woodpeckers nearly came to blows. On the 30th of August a Black man named Jim Bearfield came into Richmond from an outlying settlement. He had been wounded in the neck and hand and his face was drawn with fear. While he was in his house, somebody shot at him through an open door. According to Bearfield, he was attacked because he knew the identity of a man who was involved in the whipping of two Blacks the previous week. Bearfield swore out a warrant against H. H. Frost. Frost retaliated by suing Bearfield for perjury. Neither case ever went to court.

H. H. Frost locked the doors of his Red Hot Bar on the evening of September 3rd and was walking home when the still night was rattled by two shotgun blasts. Buckshot struck Frost in his right arm and destroyed his hat. Two days later a large assemblage met at the courthouse at which time it was determined that seven undesirable Blacks should be run out of town. Among those Blacks was a county commissioner, two schoolteachers and the district clerk. Following a little verbal sparring and an ultimatum, the seven reluctantly agreed to leave town.

Prior to the election of 1888 another barbecue was held. Jaybirds, Woodpeckers and those without political affiliation attended. The gathering, which was held at Duke's Station, ended in a confrontation between Volney Gibson (a Jaybird) and Kyle Terry (the Woodpecker candidate for county assessor). During his speech to the mixture of partisans, Terry referred to Ned Gibson as a "paper-collared dude." Volney Gibson, who was probably the best marksman in Fort Bend County, took offense to Terry's remark, and retorted, "Ned isn't here, but I'll represent him!" Kyle Terry accepted the challenge and leaped from the platform with his revolver already drawn. Members of the crowd grabbed him and trouble was averted—at least for the time being.

When the votes were counted, the Woodpeckers retained control of the county offices. Once again, it was the Black vote that decided the election. When invitations were mailed out for the Woodpeckers' victory celebration many were sent to Jaybirds. The Jaybirds remailed their invitations to Black prostitutes, an insult which infuriated the Woodpeckers. A few days later, Kyle Terry approached

Volney Gibson regarding the invitations which had been remailed by Jaybirds. If Gibson had been armed, gunplay certainly would have occurred. The incident was followed by other encounters. Kyle Terry's distaste for the Gibsons was like a fuse waiting for fire.

On the afternoon of January 21, 1889 at Wharton, as lawyer Ned Gibson walked toward the courthouse, he was dropped in his tracks by a blast from the shotgun of Kyle Terry. Ned Gibson died immediately. Although there was no immediate retaliation, the slaying was a declaration of war to the Jaybirds.

Ira Aten and his Texas Rangers attempted to intercede during the hostilities of August 16, 1889. Aten later became sheriff of Fort Bend County. *Fort Bend Museum.*

A detachment of eight Texas Rangers, led by Sergeant Ira Aten, was dispatched to Richmond to prevent further bloodshed. Several months of relative calm passed, but the town was like a powder keg just waiting for a spark to set it off. As fate would have it, four of the Rangers had been called out of town, and another lay ill in camp when all hell broke loose on August 16, 1889.

Much of the fighting occurred in front of the Fort Bend County Courthouse where several Woodpeckers had taken refuge.
Fort Bend Museum.

It was early evening as Judge J. W. Parker and his nephew, W. T. Wade, rode west on a Richmond street. Volney Gibson and his brother Guilf were riding east on the same street. As they approached each other Parker and the Gibsons drew and began shooting. Parker whirled his horse around and raced toward the courthouse. Ignoring Wade, the Gibsons gave chase. One of the slugs found its mark, hitting Parker in the back. He was able to dismount and take refuge inside the courthouse. The shots were heard by Woodpeckers, Jaybirds and others. Within moments there was a crowd in the streets. Sheriff Jim Garvey and two deputies were nearby and rushed to the aid of Parker. H. H. Frost emerged from his Brahma Bull and Red Hot Bar with a group of Jaybirds which included DeRugely Peareson, Yandell and Keane Ferris, Jeff Bryant, Charles Parnell and Will Andrus.

When he heard shots, Sergeant Ira Aten and two Rangers dashed to the scene. Aten tried to intercede but was ordered away by Sheriff Garvey. Several Woodpeckers rushed to the side of Garvey who had taken up a position behind the iron fence which separated the courthouse from the street. As the Rangers looked on helplessly, bullets flew in both directions. The leaders of each faction were the primary targets. Shots dropped both Garvey and Frost. Garvey pulled himself up, fired a couple more rounds, then fell over dead. As the former sheriff, Jake Blakely, came into sight, the wounded Frost gunned him down. Blakely died instantly. Judge Parker, whose wound had been wrapped, emerged from the door of the courthouse. As he did, a bullet from the upstairs window of the McFarlane residence hit him in the groin. Once again, Parker struggled to safety inside the courthouse. With the leaders down, the shooting finally stopped.

As previously mentioned, Garvey and Blakely were dead. Frost would die two days later. A Black girl, Robbie Smith, had been killed by a stray bullet as

The McFarlane house where three youths, Earle McFarlane, Dolph Peareson and Sid Peareson, manned the upstairs windows. From this vantage point Judge J. W. Parker was shot as he emerged from the courthouse. *Fort Bend Museum.*

the Gibsons encountered Parker (Parker and Wade were later charged in the murder). Parker would recover from his wounds. Volney Gibson, W. T. Wade, Will Andrus, Frank Schmidt and H. S. Mason also received minor injuries which would eventually mend. Following a request for the militia, Governor Ross dispatched the Houston Light Guard to Richmond as a peacekeeping force.

There were several arrests and a few lawsuits during the aftermath of the Jaybird-Woodpecker hostilities in Fort Bend County. Ira Aten became the new sheriff. Many of the Woodpeckers moved out of the area. The Jaybirds seized control of the county government, a position they would hold for many years.

The trial of Kyle Terry for the murder of Ned Gibson was set for January 21, 1890, at the courthouse in Galveston. Before ascending the steps to the criminal courtroom, Terry came face to face with Volney Gibson. Gibson drew a pistol and shot Kyle Terry in the heart. Before he could be brought to trial for killing Terry, Volney Gibson died of tuberculosis on April 9, 1891.

Richmond, Texas, in 1892. *George Memorial Library.*

Deadly killer "Deacon" Jim Miller was lynched at Ada, Oklahoma, in 1909. *University of Oklahoma Library.*

BULLETPROOF KILLER AND THE PECOS GRUDGE

James B. Miller (commonly called Jim, Deacon, or Killer Miller) was a killer for hire, whose number of victims probably equaled those of any gunfighter on the western frontier. He was an assassin who usually ambushed his prey. Miller was rarely involved in a "fair" fight.

G. A. "Bud" Frazer was a Texas Ranger and a deputy sheriff of Pecos County before his election as sheriff of Reeves County, Texas, in 1890. Miller became one of the Frazer's deputies.

An incident occurred in Reeves County which probably precipitated the bad blood between Frazer and Miller. Miller shot and killed a Mexican prisoner, then advised Frazer that he had tried to resist arrest. When the truth became known, that the prisoner had been killed because he knew that Miller had stolen a pair of mules, Bud Frazer fired him.

Miller ran against Frazer for the office of sheriff in the election of 1892, but was resoundly defeated. Shortly thereafter, Miller was appointed Pecos city marshal. The bitterness between the two grew.

Miller decided that he had had enough of Frazer and decided to assassinate him. In May 1893, Miller and two cohorts planned a scheme to stage a mock shootout at the railroad depot upon Frazer's return from a business trip. The third member of the party would shoot Frazer with a "stray" bullet from a hiding place. Somehow Frazer got wind of the plan and arrived in Pecos with two Texas Rangers.

Frazer knew that Miller would try again. But, he finally got tired of being apprehensive. On the morning of April 12, 1894, while Miller carried on a conversation in front of a Pecos hotel, Frazer approached and opened fire. His first shot hit Miller in the chest. The second struck him in his right arm as he began to draw. Miller reached around with his left hand, drew and returned the fire, but did so ineffectively as he was not left-handed. One bullet hit the ground and another struck Joe Kraus, an innocent bystander. Meanwhile, Frazer continued to fire. Three more shots hit Miller in the chest while Frazer's final shot struck him in the stomach and Miller collapsed. Thinking Miller was dead, Frazer walked off. Miller was seriously wounded, but would recover. He was wearing a steel breast plate which stopped the slugs fired at his chest.

During the election of 1894, Frazer lost his bid for re-election, then left town. He returned to Pecos on the 26th of December to settle his affairs. In front of Zimmer's Blacksmith Shop he spied Miller and drew. The gunfight that unfolded was almost a replay of the previous one. Miller took Frazer's first slug in the right arm, once again rendering the arm useless. He drew and began to shoot with his left hand. A second bullet ripped Miller's left leg. When the third and fourth hit him in the chest and he continued to stand, Frazer turned and ran. Evidently nobody had told him about the steel breast plate.

The stage was set for the third and final encounter between Miller and Frazer. The event, which occurred on September 13, 1896, was no contest. Bud Frazer was seated at a poker table in a saloon at Toyah, about twenty miles southwest of Pecos. Jim Miller stepped to the saloon door, leveled his shotgun, and killed Frazer with a load of buckshot to the head.

Deacon Jim Miller killed many over the ensuing years. It came to an end in 1909, when Miller was lynched with three others in an Ada, Oklahoma livery stable for the killing of local rancher Gus Bobbitt. Miller's last request was that his hat be placed upon his head.

The TA Ranch stable building was defended by cattlemen and Texas mercenaries during the Johnson County invasion. *Wyoming State Museum.*

THE JOHNSON COUNTY INVASION

Rustlers weren't the only folks creating a nuisance for Wyoming cattle barons. The continued growth and rising expectations of small ranch owners seemingly posed an increasing threat to their control over the cattle market. Johnson County was especially a source of irritation, for there were many small ranchers in the locale.

Hundreds of miles away, at the plush Cheyenne Club, wealthy cattlemen such as Frederick O. de Billier, his long time friend Hubert Teschemacher, Major Frank Wolcott, Fred Hesse, and William Irvine collectively contemplated an all out war against the Johnson County upstarts. The cattle barons theorized that any mere cowboy able to start a small ranch, must have acquired his stock by rustling. So, they branded the Johnson County ranchers—"rustlers." Furthermore, they agreed not to hire any cowboys who owned cattle. Pressured by the big ranchers, the state legislature passed a law which ruled that unbranded stray calves found on the range were the property of the Wyoming Stock Growers Association. The association would then sell the strays to the highest bidder. The law enraged the small ranchers because it meant that they could not claim their own strays. With the proceeds, the W.S.G.A. helped finance a private police force headed by Frank M. Canton, chief cattle detective. Canton, who was formerly sheriff of Johnson County, knew its ranchers as well as its terrain.

The outspoken Nate Champion was known to the W.S.G.A. as "King of the Rustlers," and he was high on their "black list." On November 1, 1891, near the Powder River, Frank Canton, Joe Elliott, Tom Smith, and Fred Coates converged on a line shack where Champion and a cohort, Ross Gilbertson, were living. Champion and Gilbertson were bunked in when the gunmen kicked open the door. Nate pulled his six-shooter from his gun belt draped over a bedpost. Although grazed by a slug from one of the gunmen, Champion wounded two of the intruders. The gunmen scrambled out the door and dashed for cover. Later, Champion would again meet Canton, Smith and Elliott at the KC Ranch.

In another incident, two homesteaders along the Powder River were fatally shot from ambush. Frank Canton was the prime suspect in the slayings. Provoked by the murders, the small ranchers of Johnson County established an organization called the Northern Wyoming Farmers' and Stock Growers' Association, which defied the W.S.G.A. by announcing that they would hold a roundup and retain as their own any stray calves they found. This action served as a catalyst whereby the W.S.G.A. finalized plans for their invasion of Johnson County.

The cattle barons sent Tom C. Smith, a former U.S. deputy marshal from Texas, back to his home state to enlist top gunmen. He received a fee of $2,500 for recruiting G. R. Tucker, Buck Garrett, and about twenty additional hired guns. They were paid the sum of $1,000 each. The Texans gathered at Denver, and were then transported to Cheyenne aboard a special Pullman car. There they rendezvoused with a troop of detectives and dependable ranch employees headed by Frank Canton. Horses, wagons, and supplies were readied. One hundred members of the Wyoming Stock Growers Association contributed $1,000 each to finance the invasion.

On April 5, 1892, a Union Pacific train loaded with the cattlemen, Texans, horses, wagons, and supplies, rolled out of Cheyenne bound for Casper. From Casper it was a one hundred and fifty mile ride to Buffalo, which was the Johnson County seat, the planned location for the initial attack. A snowstorm and bogged down wagons slowed the trek. Later a range detective rode in with the news that a band of rustlers was staying at the KC Ranch which was located near the Hole-in-the-Wall in Johnson County. The group voted to detour to the ranch and dispose of the rustlers before heading on to Buffalo.

Nate Champion (who had run off Frank Canton and the other gunmen a few months earlier) had recently leased the KC Ranch. Canton and his men surrounded the ranch prior to daybreak on April 9, 1892. Inside the cabin were Nate Champion,

Nick Ray (who was also on the W.S.G.A. black list), and two trappers, Ben Jones and Bill Walker, who were traveling through and had spent the night. At dawn, the trappers emerged from the cabin at different times. Each was quietly captured, then whisked away. When Ray stepped out into the morning air he was immediately dropped by rifle fire. Champion appeared and exchanged shots with the invaders as he dragged his badly wounded companion back into the cabin. Ray hung on for about two hours, then expired.

Not knowing how many men were inside, Canton was hesitant to charge the cabin. Champion sporadically exchanged gunfire with the invaders, keeping them at bay. The siege lasted for several hours. At one point, Jack Flagg and his stepson passed nearby. Flagg was on horseback, while his stepson drove a supply wagon. When they were fired upon by Canton's gunmen, Flagg cut one of the wagon's team loose for his stepson, and the two raced away to safety.

Canton's men loaded Flagg's wagon with hay, set it afire, and rolled it toward the cabin. Incredibly, through the whole ordeal, Nate Champion kept a journal in which he documented the details of the attack. His last entry was, "The house is all fired. Goodbye, boys if I never see you again." He then signed the journal as Nathan D. Champion. With the journal on his body, Champion dashed from his burning cabin with his revolvers blazing. He was dropped by a volley of gunfire and died instantly. The journal was given to *Chicago Herald* correspondent, Sam Clover, one of two newspaper reporters who accompanied the cattle barons and their men. Champion's body was left with twenty-eight bullet wounds and an attached note which read, "Cattle thieves, beware."

The invaders were careful to have had all of the telegraph wires cut leading to Buffalo. But they didn't count on the Flagg incident. From the KC Ranch, Jack Flagg and his stepson rode directly to Buffalo to warn Sheriff W. E. "Red" Angus and the citizens of Johnson County. Angus assembled a large and heavily armed posse, while riders fanned out to recruit others from throughout the county. While Sheriff Angus remained in Buffalo to help with the recruitment of reinforcements, Arapahoe Brown (who had twice been defeated in county sheriff elections) led the massive posse out to head off the invaders. Before long the posse was spotted by two of the cattle barons' outriders, who dashed back to their group with the news. During a period of confusion and indecision, Major Frank Wolcott assumed command of the cattlemen. Realizing that the trail to Buffalo was impassable, Wolcott ordered a barbed-wire fence cut then turned his forces toward the friendly confines of the TA Ranch, located about fourteen miles from Buffalo. The ranch was nestled on an inside bend of Crazy Woman Creek. The ranch house, stable, and a couple of outbuildings were surrounded by log and barbed-wire fences, and appeared to be fairly defensible. Approximately fifty yards west of the stable, Wolcott instructed some of the men to build a small log fort from which several sharpshooters could cover the west side of the ranch. The small fortification, which was constructed on a knoll, measured about 12 x 14 feet. Breastworks were erected and trenches dug as the cattlemen worked all day, and into the night, to strengthen their defenses. As the sun rose on the morning of April the 11th, the cattlemen could see that they were surrounded. Arapahoe Brown's posse had also dug in prior to dawn, with men stationed across Crazy Woman Creek on three sides of the ranch, and across every rise to the west. They were busy constructing breastworks, as well. The Johnson County force numbered about ninety at dawn, but swelled to over three hundred as the day wore on. Shooting was mild—just enough to keep the invaders pinned down —while reinforcements continued to arrive. It also allowed them time to construct a "rolling" breastworks, from the wheels of the invaders' abandoned supply wagons. Arapahoe Brown's plan was to close in on the TA buildings behind the rolling breastworks until they were close enough to lob dynamite at the buildings.

With the telegraph wires repaired on April the 12th (the second day of the siege), the Buffalo telegrapher was able to send a wire to Governor Amos Barber advising him of the invasion and requesting troops to assist in the capture of the cattle barons. Barber had known all along of the invasion plans and favored the big ranchers who helped support his campaign. He chose to do nothing until he received some word from the cattlemen. Later in the day, when he fully understood the gravity of the situation, Barber wired President Benjamin Harrison asking for assistance from the U.S. Army.

Meanwhile, the ladies of Buffalo prepared and sent wagon loads of food to the Johnson County troops, while the invaders at the TA Ranch ate potatoes. As their hopes dimmed, tensions rose, and many of the cattlemen began feuding with one another.

At daybreak, on April the 13th, the Johnson County forces put their plan into action. The rolling breastworks began to creep down the hill toward the TA buildings.

The timing couldn't have been more amazing. Within minutes of all-out war, three troops of U.S. Cavalry appeared over the rise. Colonel J. J. Vanhorn, detachment commander, announced to Sheriff Angus that they were under Presidential order to take charge of the men inside the ranch buildings and to safely escort them to jail. Major Wolcott was called out to meet with Vanhorn and Sheriff Angus. Wolcott agreed to surrender to the cavalry. The cattle barons and their men were placed under military arrest, then led away to Fort McKinney, while hundreds of Johnson County citizens watched.

The prisoners, who were charged with the murders of Nate Champion and Nick Ray, were moved to Fort Russell, at Cheyenne, where they remained for ten weeks. Insisting that the prisoners would not receive a fair trial in Buffalo, a

Following their defeat by Johnson County citizens, the Wyoming cattle barons and hired Texas gunfighters are shown in custody at Fort Russell. Frank Canton is seated at the extreme right (second row) and Major Wolcott is standing just behind Canton's left shoulder. *Wyoming State Museum.*

judge ruled that the venue be changed to Cheyenne. No longer a Federal matter, the prisoners were moved once more—this time to an auditorium in Cheyenne. The same judge stipulated that Johnson County shall pay for their confinement —at a cost of $100 per day, per man. Shortly thereafter, the Johnson County Treasury went broke and the judge ordered the prisoners released without bond. Later, with prosecution hopeless, Johnson County authorities dropped the criminal charges against the invaders.

Afterwards, Major Frank Wolcott reflected on the siege at the TA Ranch. He said, "We only figured on fighting rustlers, and we were willing to take all chances of a war with them. Their ability to enlist aid amazed and stunned me. The whole country turned out to whip us, and they almost did it."

Chauncey Dewey was the central figure in the Dewey-Berry feud.
Kansas State Historical Society.

THE DEWEY-BERRY FEUD

Cheyenne County, in the northwestern corner of Kansas, was the scene of a bloody encounter on June 3, 1903. The gunfight which occurred that afternoon was the culmination of several years of strained relationships. The vendetta would continue in the courtroom for many years thereafter. The fight, which had its roots in land and cattle, was known as the Dewey-Berry Feud.

Following the great Chicago fire of 1871, C. P. and A. P. Dewey became extremely wealthy through real estate speculations. The brothers reinvested their fortune in mortgages and consequently became richer. Northwestern Kansas land, which previously had little value, came into demand in 1885 causing real estate values to jump considerably. The Dewey brothers offered loans of from $700 to $1000 on quarter sections which they would hold as security. The land boom dissipated and the economy became rough in 1887. The Deweys foreclosed on several thousand acres of land, predominately in Cheyenne, Rawlins, Sherman, Thomas and Decatur Counties.

As the cattle business flourished during the late 1890s, C. P. Dewey became more interested in investing in Kansas. The interests of A. P. Dewey lay elsewhere, so the brothers divided their holdings and went their separate ways. During a period of financial depression between 1893 and 1897, settlers found it difficult to pay taxes on their land. C. P. Dewey cut a deal with several counties whereby they would accept a payment of approximately fifty percent for the taxes due. Dewey would pay the taxes and take tax deeds (or tax liens) on those specific properties. Basically he worked every angle he could to obtain property at the "right" price.

C. P. Dewey established a cattle ranch in the southwestern corner of Rawlins County. Its land extended into Thomas, Sherman and Cheyenne Counties. He dubbed it Oak Ranch. Its 40,000 acres were approximately half of his Kansas holdings. The ambitious Dewey wanted Oak Ranch to become the largest in the state of Kansas. Dewey, who continued to make his home in Chicago, placed his son, Chauncey, in charge of Oak Ranch. C. P. Dewey invested in other areas of Kansas, as well. He purchased a large tract of land in Riley County where he constructed a lakefront resort. Manhattan Beach, on Eureka Lake, was located near the town of Manhattan.

Chauncey Dewey was refined, well educated and had all the polish of an eastern gentleman. He was straight forward, looked a man right in the eye when he talked to him, and was well liked by his employees. The cowboys at Oak Ranch appreciated Chauncey because he "led by example." He had the culture of an Easterner, but also the horsemanship, marksmanship and ranch savvy of a Westerner. Chauncey, who was in his early 20s when he operated Oak Ranch, was ambitious like his father, but he often took less than desirable means to achieve an end.

Dewey obtained title to as much land as possible. He not only fenced his property but ran miles and miles of wire across open range virtually boxing in many small landowners. This enraged the settlers because they couldn't keep cattle without the use of grazing land. Dewey claimed that the fences were designed to keep his cattle out of settlers' crops.

Furthermore, Chauncey Dewey continued to purchase more land. When settlers refused to sell, they would often become isolated when Dewey purchased all of the land surrounding them. By 1901 the situation had become very tense. Believing that a fight was inevitable, settlers armed themselves to the teeth. So too did Dewey's riders.

The settlers were led by a family named Berry. Their resentment toward C. P. and Chauncey Dewey originated years earlier when the Deweys foreclosed on the Berry homestead which had a past-due mortgage. When the Berrys refused to move, Dewey took out a court order for their eviction, which was carried out by the sheriff. The Berrys relocated to a property which they leased in Cheyenne County, very close to the boundary of Oak Ranch.

In 1901, Daniel P. Berry was a stout, heavily-bearded man age 60. His wife, Harriett M. "Hattie" Berry would later be a thorn in the side of Chauncey Dewey. Nearby were the residences of Daniel's sons, Alpheus W., Beach D. and Burchard B. Berry. A nephew, William Roy Berry lived a short distance to the east in Rawlins County. They were a tough bunch and very determined to stand their ground against the men from Oak Ranch. The Berrys weren't without skeletons in their closets either. In 1891, Daniel, Alpheus (his eldest son) and Beach were involved in horse stealing in Colorado. Warrants were issued for the arrest of all three, with Alpheus ultimately taking the rap in order to get his father and brother off the hook. He spent several months in the Colorado state penitentiary at Cañon City.

Several altercations occurred between the Dewey and Berry factions beginning in April of 1902. One afternoon as the Berrys were sowing a section of land in barley, Chauncey Dewey and William J. McBride confronted them and advised the settlers that they were farming on Dewey property. At gunpoint Burchard Berry ordered them to leave the premises—and they did. From the courts, Chauncey Dewey obtained a restraining order to keep the Berrys off his property and away from Oak Ranch employees. Dewey had Roy Berry arrested for disturbing the peace, and then had warrants issued against Beach and Burchard for assault. The enraged settlers decided that enough was enough. They organized a committee to confront Chauncey Dewey with their demands. On two separate occasions they sent a large contingency to Oak Ranch in an effort to do so, but both times Chauncey Dewey was out of town. On the 18th of July, 1902, nineteen armed settlers, including the Berrys, confronted Chauncey Dewey with their demands. Burchard Berry advised that if Dewey did not withdraw the warrants against the Berrys immediately that there would be retaliation. Two days later when the warrants had not been withdrawn, eleven of Dewey's thoroughbred bulls were killed, a pasture was torched, fences destroyed and several wells were trashed. On another occasion, Daniel Berry accused Dewey and his men of firing several shots through the Berry house one night. Dewey denied the allegation. Refusing to be fenced in, the Berrys would cut the wire fences and allow their cattle to roam on Dewey pastures.

Threats and counter threats were passed back and forth for several months. The situation was like a powder keg waiting for someone to light the fuse. Both factions had excellent marksmen. Not only was Chauncey a crack shot, but several of his employees were also. William J. McBride was considered the best shot at Oak Ranch. The former soldier could drop jackrabbits on the run with a rifle. Another of Dewey's marksmen was Clyde Wilson who also was a soldier and served for a while as assistant city marshal at Salina. It is said that Burchard Berry could shatter an egg thrown high into the air with either a pistol or rifle.

Chauncey Dewey had sued the Berrys for unpaid rent on a quarter section of Oak Ranch land which the Berrys had been using. A judgment was issued in Dewey's favor in the amount of $35. The sheriff seized (by levy) one windmill and one watertank. Furthermore, he scheduled an auction to be held at the Berry's property on June 2, 1903, in order to dispose of these items. On the day of the sale, three Oak Ranch employees rode to the residence of Alpheus Berry to attend the proceedings. Albert Winship was accompanied by Will Day and Tom LeBow, a Dewey foreman. Burchard Berry approached the trio and ordered them to stay off Berry property. When the sheriff and auctioneer arrived, Winship was allowed to enter the premises in order to bid on the watertank which he ultimately purchased for $5. Winship was advised that he could return to pick up the tank. As he, Day and LeBow began to depart they were confronted by Burchard, Beach and Roy Berry. A heated argument ensued which included more threats. There was no fight but it was forthcoming.

Realizing that there might be trouble when they retrieved the watertank, Chauncey Dewey suggested they take a large armed force to the residence of Alpheus Berry. Ten heavily armed Oak Ranch riders headed toward the Berry place on the afternoon of June 3rd. Chauncey Dewey was accompanied by Albert Winship, William J. McBride, Clyde Wilson, Charles Wilson, Thomas O'Neill, Benjamin F. Slater, James Armentrout, Frederick Dye and Edward Tucker. Two of the men rode in a wagon while the other eight were on horseback. When they arrived at the Alpheus Berry house, McBride went to the door to ask permission to load the watertank. Daniel was dining with Viola Berry (Alpheus' wife) and her three children. Viola went to the door and gave McBride permission to load the tank. Daniel, who was reputedly unarmed, walked outside to observe. Within moments Alpheus arrived from a neighbor's house and joined his father. He was also allegedly unarmed. Dewey's men were in the process of draining the tank when Burchard, Beach and Roy Berry approached on horseback. They drew to a halt, dismounted, then tied up their horses. They turned and walked toward the tank. Gunfire suddenly erupted. Witnesses for each side later contended that the other shot first. A bullet from Chauncey Dewey's Savage rifle shattered the jaw and ear of Roy Berry. He fell to the ground. McBride fired his Winchester with deadly aim. His bullet struck Burchard Berry in the head. He was killed instantly. Daniel Berry was shot in the stomach and dropped to the ground, dead. Alpheus and Beach Berry turned to run for cover. Another bullet immediately struck Alpheus in the back of the head. He was also dead. Another bullet nicked Beach Berry in one leg as he scampered to safety. Although wounded, Roy Berry was still alive and attempted to crawl to shelter when two more bullets whistled through his felt hat. He dropped on his stomach and lay motionless feigning death. When the smoke cleared, Daniel, Alpheus and Burchard Berry were all dead. Beach Berry and his cousin Roy were wounded. A horse had also been killed by a stray bullet. After the Oak Ranch bunch departed unscathed, Roy and Beach mounted their horses and rode in separate directions. Roy headed to the home of his friend Lemuel Capron to receive assistance for his wound. Beach spurred his horse in the direction of Bird City to wire for the sheriff and coroner.

Mobs seeking vigilante justice quickly gathered at St. Francis and the Berry ranch. Beach Berry was only able to identify three of the Dewey men as having actually done the shooting—Chauncey Dewey, W. J. McBride and Clyde Wilson. Sheriff Robert McCullough and Deputy Sheriff E. B. Robertson rounded up a posse and rode to Oak Ranch on the evening of the 3rd. They received a cordial reception. Dewey agreed that he, McBride and Wilson would submit to arrest if the sheriff could guarantee them protection from the mobs. McCullough placed the trio under arrest and left them in the custody of Robertson while he rode to St. Francis to wire the Governor for additional help. Governor Bailey responded by sending the Osborne Militia (Company G, 2nd Regiment, National Guard) commanded by Captain V. E. Cunningham to assist Sheriff McCullough. A preliminary hearing was scheduled in St. Francis, a town which had no jailhouse. Word had spread that a mob planned to lynch Dewey, McBride and Wilson, and burn Oak Ranch to the ground. The presence of the Osborne Militia seemed to quell most of the harsh talk. However, eventually Sheriff McCullough and the militia (a force of 54 heavily-armed men) moved their prisoners to a temporary camp at St. Francis for the hearing which commenced on June 15th.

In a shrewd move, Dewey's attorneys filed an application for the writ of habeas corpus in the Kansas Supreme Court requesting bail for their clients. A hearing was set at the state capitol in Topeka. Sheriff A. T. "Bert" Lucas left Topeka (acting as a special marshal of the state Supreme Court) en route to Cheyenne County where he would pick up the prisoners. The Osborne Militia would accompany them on their trip to Topeka. This legal action moved the accused men far from the mobs in Cheyenne County. If Dewey had sought bail in Cheyenne County, and had it granted, he might have been freed, without protection, in a dangerous and hostile environment. Bail was granted at Topeka and the accused men left for C. P. Dewey's resort at Eureka Lake to await trial. Liberty was granted under bonds of $15,000 each furnished by C. P. Dewey and two of his friends.

The much publicized trial of Chauncey Dewey, William J. McBride and Clyde Wilson for the murder of Burchard Berry opened on February 2, 1904 in the Norton County district court. After a bitterly contested trial, the jury deliberated for twenty-eight and one-half hours before returning a verdict (on March 19, 1904) of not guilty. Their decision was highly unpopular. Four days later the twelve jurors were hanged in effigy from different trees in the courthouse yard at Norton. Each of the figures, which were comprised of old clothes stuffed with hay, bore the name of a juror. An old man wandered about the streets carrying with him a hangman's noose. He claimed he was looking for a Dewey man, just any Dewey man.

C. P. Dewey's wife (who was not Chauncey's mother) sued for divorce. On June 10, 1904 C. P. Dewey died. His will was highly contested. Chauncey Dewey sold Oak Ranch, and then married the daughter of an Episcopal Bishop in 1908.

The Berrys finally received some retribution from Chauncey Dewey. Following civil suits which were filed in 1905, Harriet M. Berry and William Roy Berry were awarded (in 1918) damages in the amounts of $7,140 and $1,585.35 respectfully. Dewey appealed the decrees to the Supreme Court which upheld the damages.

The Dewey-Berry feud culminated at the home of Alpheus Berry on June 3, 1903. Although the origin of these photographs is unknown, they are apparently accurate and were admitted into evidence at two trials. Daniel and Alpheus Berry were killed near the carcass of Chauncey Dewey's horse, while Roy (wounded) and Burchard (killed) were shot down beyond the sod wall. *Kansas State Historical Society.*

Acknowledgements

Nancy Flanders
Ruth S. Bennett
Teresa Bond
Sue Anderson
Oklahoma Historical Society
Archives & Manuscripts Division of the Oklahoma Historical Society
David N. Kloppenborg, Boot Hill Museum
Jeanette Steinkuehler, Cimarron Library
Kirk Anderson, *The Jacksonian*, Cimarron
Kathleen Holt
Maurice Johnson
Christie Stanley, Kansas State Historical Society
Bill Hubbs, The Barney Hubbs Collection
LaVaughn Bresnahan, Wyoming State Museum
Bob Chandler, Wells Fargo Historical Services
Center for American History, University of Texas at Austin
John R. Lovett, Western History Collections, University of Oklahoma Library
John W. Anderson, Archives, Texas State Library
University of New Mexico, Zimmerman Library
Museum of New Mexico
Arizona State University, Hayden Library
Bruce Hanson, Western History Department, Denver Public Library
The Wild Horse Collection
Robert G. McCubbin, The Robert G. McCubbin Collection
Lee Good and Sandra Thompson, J. M. Davis Arms & Historical Museum
El Paso Museum of History
UTEP Library, University of Texas at El Paso
Western Heritage Museum, Union Pacific Railroad Collection
Doug Wickland, National Firearms Museum
Nancy Sherbert, Kansas State Historical Society
Jane Hoerster, Mason County Library
Grace Rae Davenport
Don DeCoss, Wells Fargo Museum
Dawn L. Rodrigues, California State Library
Byron Johnson and Christina Stopka, Texas Ranger Museum
Arizona State University, University Archives
Jim Bradshaw, Nita Stewart Haley Memorial Library and J. Evetts
Haley History Center
Mario M. Einaudi, Arizona Historical Society
Hayes Colburn

Molly Freeman, Austin Public History Center
Mary Nelson, Special Collections, Wichita State University
W. M. Von-Maszewski and Debbie Shoemaker, George Memorial Library
Peter Blodgett, Huntington Library
Mary McKinstry
Patsy Goebel
Elizabeth Kelly Brautigam
Keystone Square Museum
Amy Johns, Fort Bend Museum
John Allwright
Elvis Fleming and Annette Lucero, Historical Center for
    Southeast New Mexico
Sarah Harrison Cobb
Beverly Hammond and Drew Gomber, Lincoln Heritage Trust
Barbara Smith-LaBorde, University of Texas at Austin
Jodi Wright-Gidley, Bell County Museum
Berneta Peoples and Gene Bigham, Belton Journal
Bena Taylor Kirkscey
George Anne Cormier, Calhoun County Museum
Connie Todd, Southwest Texas State University
Lynda Hatch
Vircenoy Macatee and Nevin Foster, Hood County Museum
Anna Crawford
Ben Evridge, Comanche County Museum
Lena Armstrong, Belton City Library
Mutsu Crumley
Lampasas County Historical Commission
Deborah Bond
Austin Public Library
Norlin Library, University of Colorado at Boulder

Bibliography

BOOKS

Adams, Ramon F. *A Fitting Death for Billy the Kid.* Norman: University of Oklahoma Press, 1960.

Adams, Ramon F. *Six-Guns & Saddle Leather: A Bibliography of Books & Pamphlets on Western Outlaws and Gunmen.* Norman: University of Oklahoma Press, 1969.

Ashbaugh, Don. *Nevada's Turbulent Yesterday.* Los Angeles: Westernlore Press, 1963.

Ballert, Marion, with Carl W. Breihan. *Billy the Kid: A Date with Destiny.* Seattle: Superior Publishing Co., 1970.

Bartholomew, Ed. *Wyatt Earp: The Man & the Myth.* Toyahvale, TX: Frontier Book Co., 1964.

Beebe, Lucius, and Charles Clegg. *U.S. West: The Saga of Wells Fargo.* New York: E. P. Dutton & Co. 1949.

Block, Eugene B. *Great Train Robberies of the West.* New York: Coward-McCann, Inc., 1959.

Boyer, Glenn G. *Wyatt Earp's Tombstone Vendetta.* Honolulu, HI: Talei Publishers, 1993.

Brown, John Henry. *History of Texas, From 1685 to 1892. Volume One.* St. Louis, MO: Becktold & Co., 1892.

Calvert, Robert A. and Arnoldo De León. *The History of Texas. Second Edition.* Wheeling, IL: Harlan Davidson, Inc., 1996.

Chamblin, Thomas S., ed. *The Historical Encyclopedia of Texas.* Austin: The Texas Historical Institute, 1982.

Coe, George W. *Frontier Fighter.* Albuquerque: University of New Mexico Press, 1934.

Coolidge, Dane. *Fighting Men of the West.* New York: E.P. Dutton, 1932.

Dedera, Don. *A Little War of Our Own: The Pleasant Valley Feud Revisited.* Flagstaff, AZ: Northland Press, 1987.

Dimsdale, Thomas J. *The Vigilantes of Montana.* Norman: University of Oklahoma Press, 1953.

Douglas, C. L. *Famous Texas Feuds.* Austin: State House Press, 1988.

Ellison, Glenn. *Cowboys Under the Mogollon Rim.* Tucson: University of Arizona Press, 1968.

Elman, Robert. *Badmen of the West.* Scaucus, NJ: Ridge Press, Inc., 1974.

Erwin, Allen A. *The Southwest of John H. Slaughter, 1841-1922: Pioneer Cattleman and Traildriver of Texas, the Pecos, and Arizona and Sheriff of Tombstone.* Glendale, CA: Arthur II. Clark Co., 1965.

Ewell, Thomas T. History of Hood County. Granbury, TX: Frank Gaston, Publisher, 1895. Reprinted by the Junior Woman's Club, Granbury, TX, 1956.

Faulk, Odie B. *Land of Many Frontiers, a History of the American Southwest.* New York: Oxford University Press, 1968.

Forrest, Earle R. *Arizona's Dark and Bloody Ground.* Caldwell, ID: Caxton Printers, 1952.

Fuller, Henry Clay. *A Texas Sheriff.* Nacogdoches, TX: Baker Printing Co., 1931.

Garavaglia, Louis A. and Charles G. Worman. *Firearms of the American West, 1803-1865.* Albuquerque: University of New Mexico Press, 1984.

Garavaglia, Louis A. and Charles G. Worman. *Firearms of the American West, 1866-1894.* Albuquerque: University of New Mexico Press, 1985.

Gard, Wayne. *Frontier Justice.* Norman: University of Oklahoma Press, 1949.

Garrett, Patrick F. *The Authentic Life of Billy, the Kid: The Noted Desperado of the Southwest, Whose Deeds of Daring and Blood Made His Name a Terror in New Mexico, Arizona, and Northern Mexico.* Norman: University of Oklahoma Press, 1954.

Graves, Richard S. *Oklahoma Outlaws: A Graphic History of the Early Days of Oklahoma.* Oklahoma City: State Printing Co.,1915.

Grimes, Roy. *300 Years In Victoria County.* Victoria, TX: The Victoria Advocate Publishing Co., 1968

Hamlin, William Lee. *The True Story of Billy the Kid.* Caldwell, ID: Caxton Printers, Ltd., 1959.

Hardin, John Wesley. *The Life of John Wesley Hardin as Written by Himself.* Norman: University of Oklahoma Press, 1961.

Hertzog, Peter. *A Dictionary of New Mexico Desperadoes.* Santa Fe, NM: Press of the Territorian, 1965.

Horan, James D. *Across the Cimarron.* New York: Crown Publishers, Inc., 1956.

Horan, James D. *The Authentic Wild West: The Gunfighters.* New York: Crown Publishers, Inc., 1976.

Horan, James D. *Desperate Men: Revelations from the Sealed Pinkerton Files.* Garden City, NY: Doubleday and Co., Inc., 1962.

Hunter, J. Marvin and Noah H. Rose. *The Album of Gunfighters.* San Antonio: Hunter and Rose, 1951.

Jahns, Pat. *The Frontier World of Doc Holliday.* New York: Hastings House, 1957.

James, Vinton Lee. *Frontier and Pioneer Recollections of Early Days in San Antonio and West Texas.* San Antonio: Vinton Lee James, 1938.

Jennings, N.A. *A Texas Ranger.* New York: Charles Scribner's Sons, 1899.

Lake, Stuart N. *Wyatt Earp: Frontier Marshal.* Boston and New York: Houghton Mifflin, 1931.
Lamar, Howard R. (Ed.). *The Reader's Encyclopedia of the American West.* New York: Thomas Y. Crowell Co., 1977.
Langford, N.P. *Vigilante Days and Ways.* Missoula, MT: Montana State University, 1957.
Larson, T.A. *History of Wyoming.* Lincoln: University of Nebraska Press, 1965.
Llewellyn, Karl N., and E. Adamson Hoebel. *The Cheyenne Way: Conflict and Case Law in Primitive Jurisprudence.* Norman: University of Oklahoma Press, 1941.
Lucia, Ellis. *Tough Men, Tough Country.* Englewood Cliffs, NJ: Prentice-Hall, Inc., 1963.
Malone, Dumas, ed. *Dictionary of American Biography.* New York: Charles Scribner's Sons, 1943.
Malone, Michael P. and Richard B. Roeder. *Montana: A History of Two Centuries.* Seattle: University of Washington Press, 1988.
McNeal, T.A. *When Kansas Was Young.* New York: The Macmillan Co., 1922.
McReynolds, Edwin C. *Oklahoma: A History of The Sooner State.* Norman: University of Oklahoma Press, 1954.
Metz, Leon C. *John Selman, Gunfighter.* Norman: University of Oklahoma Press, 1980.
Metz, Leon C. *Pat Garrett: The Story of a Western Lawman.* Norman: University of Oklahoma Press, 1973.
Miller, Floyd. *Bill Tilghman: Marshal of the Last Frontier.* New York: Doubleday and Co., Inc., 1968.
Miller, Nyle H., and Joseph W. Snell. *Great Gunfighters of the Kansas Cowtowns, 1867-1886.* Lincoln: University of Nebraska Press, 1967.
Nash, Jay Robert. *Encyclopedia of Western Lawmen & Outlaws.* New York: Paragon House, 1992.
Nolan, Frederick. *Bad Blood: The Life and Times of the Horrell Brothers.* Stillwater, OK: Barbed Wire Press, 1994.
Nolan, Frederick. *The Lincoln County War: A Documentary History.* Norman: University of Oklahoma Press, 1992.
Nordyke, Lewis. *John Wesley Hardin: Texas Gunman.* New York: William Morrow & Co., 1957.
Olmstead, Frederick Law. *A Journey Through Texas; or, a Saddle-trip on the Southwestern Frontier: with a Statistical Appendix.* New York: Dix, Edwards and Co., 1857.
O'Neal, Bill. *Encyclopedia of Western Gunfighters.* Norman: University of Oklahoma Press, 1979.
Parsons, Chuck and Marjorie. *Bowen and Hardin.* College Station, TX: Creative Publishing Co., 1991.

Patterson, Richard. *Historical Atlas of the Outlaw West*. Boulder, CO: Johnson Books, 1985.

Patterson, Richard. *Wyoming's Outlaw Days*. Boulder, CO: Johnson Books, 1982.

Poe, John William. *The Death of Billy the Kid*. Boston and New York: Houghton Mifflin Co., 1933.

Polk, Stella Gipson. *Mason and Mason County: A History*. Austin: The Pemberton Press, 1966.

Prassel, Frank Richard. *The Western Peace Officer: A Legacy of Law and Order*. Norman: University of Oklahoma Press, 1972.

Raine, William MacLeod. *Famous Sheriffs and Western Outlaws*. New York: New Home Library, 1944.

Rennert, Vincent Paul. *Western Outlaws*. New York: Crowell-Collier Press, 1968.

Rosa, Joseph G. *Age of the Gunfighter: Men and Weapons on the Frontier 1840-1900*. Norman: University of Oklahoma Press, 1995.

Rose, Victor M. *The Texas Vendetta, or the Sutton-Taylor Feud*. Houston: Frontier Press of Texas, 1956.

Schultz, Vernon B. *Southwestern Town: The Story of Willcox, Arizona*. Tucson: University of Arizona Press, 1964.

Shirley, Glenn. *Shotgun for Hire: The Story of "Deacon" Jim Miller, Killer of Pat Garrett*. Norman: University of Oklahoma Press, 1970.

Sonnichsen, C.L. *I'll Die Before I'll Run*. New York: The Devin-Adair Co., 1962.

Sonnichsen, C.L. *Outlaw. Bill Mitchell alias Baldy Russell. His Life and Times*. Denver: Sage Books, 1965.

Sonnichsen, C.L. *Ten Texas Feuds*. Albuquerque: University of New Mexico Press, 1957.

Steckmesser, Kent Ladd. *The Western Hero in History and Legend*. Norman: University of Oklahoma Press, 1965.

Stiles, T.J. *In Their Own Words: Warriors and Pioneers*. New York: The Berkley Publishing Group, 1996

Summerfield, Charles. [Alfred W. Arrington]. *The Desperadoes of the Southwest: containing an account of the Cane-Hill murders, together with the lives of several of the most notorious regulators and moderators of that region*. New York: W.H. Graham, 1847.

Sutton, Fred Ellsworth. *Hands Up!: Stories of the Six-Gun Fighters of the Old Wild West*. As told to A.B. McDonald. Indianapolis: Bobbs-Merrill, 1927.

Sutton, Robert C., Jr. *The Sutton-Taylor Feud*. Quanah, TX: Nortex Press, 1974.

Thrapp, Dan L. *Encyclopedia of Frontier Biography: Vols I, II, III, IV*. Lincoln: University of Nebraska Press, 1988.

Tilghman, Zoe A. *Marshal of the Last Frontier: Life and Services of William Matthew (Bill) Tilghman for 50 years one of the greatest peace officers of the West.* Glendale, CA: Arthur H. Clark Co.,1964.
Trachtman, Paul. ed. *The Gunfighters.* New York: Time-Life Books, 1974.
U.S. Bureau of the Census, Revised by the Social Science Research Council. *The Statistical History of the United States from Colonial Times to the Present.* Stanford: Fairfield Publishers, Inc., 1965.
Waters, Frank. *The Earp Brothers of Tombstone.* London: Neville Spearman, Ltd., 1962.
Webb, Walter Prescott. *The Great Plains.* New York: Grosset and Dunlap, 1931.
Webb, Walter Prescott. *The Texas Rangers: A Century of Frontier Defense.* Boston: Houghton Mifflin Co., 1935.
Webb, Walter Prescott. *The Texas Rangers: A Century of Frontier Defense.* Austin, University of Texas Press, 1965.
Wellman, Paul I. *A Dynasty of Western Outlaws.* Garden City, NY: Doubleday and Co., Inc., 1961.
Wharton, Clarence Ray. *Wharton's History of Fort Bend County.* San Antonio: The Naylor Co., 1939.
Wilson, Neill Compton. *Treasure Express: Epic Days of the Wells Fargo.* New York: Macmillan, 1936.
Ziegler, J. A. *Wave of the Gulf.* San Antonio: The Naylor Co., 1938.

NEWSPAPERS

Austin Weekly Statesman
Albuquerque Review
Arizona Champion (Flagstaff, AZ)
Arizona Citizen/Daily Citizen (Tucson, AZ)
Bastrop Advertiser (Bastrop, The)
Champion (Norton, KS)
Daily Citizen (Tucson, AZ)
Daily Free Press (Atchison, KS)
Dallas News
Dallas Daily Herald
Dallas Times-Herald
Denver Post
El Paso Evening Post
El Paso Times
Ford County Globe (Dodge City, KS)
Galveston Daily News/Galveston News
Gonzales Enquirer
Grant County Herald (Silver City, NM)
Herald (San Francisco, CA)

Houston Chronicle
Houston Post/Houston Daily Post
Houston Telegraph
Jacksonian, The (Cimarron, KS)
Journal-Miner (Prescott, AZ)
Julesburg Advocate
Kansas City Journal
Kansas City Star
Kansas City Times
Larned Press, The
Las Cruces Rio Grande Republican
Lincoln County Leader
Mesilla Valley Independent (Las Cruces, NM)
Oklahoma State Capital (Oklahoma City, OK)
Omaha Republican
Pawnee Herald (Larned, KS)
Prescott Courier
Richmond Democrat (Richmond, TX)
Richmond Opinion (Richmond, TX)
Roswell Daily Record
Rocky Mountain News (Denver, CO)
Sacramento Times
San Antonio Daily Express
San Antonio Daily Herald
San Francisco Call
San Saba Daily News
Santa Fe New Mexican
Tombstone Epitaph
Topeka Capital
Topeka Commonwealth
Topeka Journal
Victoria Advocate
Wichita Eagle

ARTICLES

Aten, Ira. "Six and One-Half Years in the Ranger Service." *Frontier Times,* (February, 1945).

Barnes, Will C. "The Pleasant Valley War of 1887." *Arizona Historical Review,* Vol. 4, Nos. 3, 4, The Arizona Pioneer's Historical Society, October 1931, January, 1932.

Bocock, Pamela S. "Camp Guthrie: Urban Outpost in the Territory, 1889-1891." *Chronicles of Oklahoma,* 1984 62(2): 166-189.

Carlson, Paul H. "Panhandle Pastores: Early Sheepherding in the Texas Panhandle." *Panhandle-Plains Historical Review,* 1980 53: 1-15.

Cawelti, John G. "The Gunfighter and Society," *The American West,* Vol. V, No. 2 (March 1968), 30-35, 76-78.

Clum, John P. "It Happened in Tombstone," *Arizona Historical Review,* Vol. II, No. 3 (October 1929), 46-72.

Cline, Don. "Secret Life of Billy the Kid." *True West,* April 1984.

Dedera, Don. "They Died with Their Boots On—The Pleasant Valley War Revisited," *Arizona Highways Magazine,* August 1984.

Holden, W. C. "Law and Lawlessness on the Texas Frontier, 1875-1890," *Southwestern Historical Quarterly,* Vol. XLIV, No. 2 (October 1940), 188-203.

Hooper, Mildred and C.R. Hooper. "Pleasant Valley: an Unpleasant Past," *Outdoor Arizona Magazine,* August 1974.

Johnson, Jo. "Commodore Perry Owens," *Arizona Highways Magazine,* October 1960.

Kilman, Ed. "Jaybird vs. Woodpecker War." Houston *Chronicle,* April 9, 1944.

Koop, Waldo E., "Enter John Wesley Hardin, A Dim Trail to Abilene." *The Prairie Scout,* Vol. II, ed. by The Westerners. Ives Printing Co., 1974.

McGinty, Brian. "John Wesley Hardin: Gentleman of Guns." *American History Illustrated,* Summer 1982.

Rasch, P. J. "The Horrell War." *New Mexico Historical Review,* Vol. 31 (July, 1956), 223-231.

Rohrs, Richard C. "The Study of Oklahoma History During the Territorial Period: An Alternative Methodological Approach." *Chronicles of Oklahoma,* 1982 60(2): 174-185.

Sanchez, Lynda A. "They Loved Billy the Kid." *True West,* January 1984.

Simmons, Marc. "Billy the Kid and the Lincoln County War." *American History Illustrated,* Summer 1982.

Weiss, Harold J., Jr. "Western Lawmen: Image and Reality." *Journal of the West,* 1985 24(1): 23-32.

Woody, Clara T., and Milton L. Schwartz. "War in Pleasant Valley: The Outbreak of the Graham-Tewksbury Feud." *The Journal of Arizona History,* Vol. 18, Issue 1 (1977), 43-68.

OTHER SOURCES

Barnes, Will C. *Biography of Commodore Perry Owens.*
Arizona Historical Society - transcript
Tucson (no date)

Colorado State Archives, Denver, CO:
Calvert, Charles E., "United States Marshals: Territorial and State."

Federal Records Center, Denver, CO:
   Criminal Dockets, First Judicial District, New Mexico Territory, August 1, 1882-March 26, 1912.
   Records of the U.S. District Court, Territory of New Mexico, Fifth Judicial District, 1890-1911.
   Records of the U.S. District Court, Territory of New Mexico. First Judicial District, 1896-1909.

Flake, Osmer D. *Some Reminiscenses of the Pleasant Valley War and Causes That Led Up to It*, typescript edited by Levi S. Udall, Arizona State Department of Library, Archives and Public Records, received April 13, 1958.

Huntington Library, San Marino, CA:
   Overland Mail Collection

Kansas State Historical Society, Topeka, KS:
   Biography Scrapbooks

Robert G., McCubbin Collection, El Paso, TX

Lincoln County, N.M.: Estate Records, Contracts and Leases

National Archives and Records Administration, Washington, D.C.:
   Civil War Records, Post Returns, Pensions, Headstone Applications, Volunteer Service Files, Census (1850 on)

Oklahoma Historical Society, Oklahoma City, OK:
   Foreman, Grant — U.S. Marshal, Vertical File.
   Indian-Pioneer History (W.P.A. Project, 1937).

United States Geological Survey, Maps, U.S. Department of the Interior, Federal Center, Denver.

University of Arizona Archives, Tucson, AZ:
   Slaughter, [John], Manuscript File.

University of Oklahoma Archives, Norman, OK:
   Tilghman, [Mr. and Mrs.] William, Manuscript File.

University of Wyoming, Western History Center, Laramie, WY:
   Canton, Frank M., Manuscript File.
   LeFors, Joe, Manuscript File.

University of Texas at Austin, The Center for American History and The Eugene C. Barker Texas History Center, Special Collections.

Wichita State University, Special Collections

Wild Horse Collection, Round Rock, TX

Index

A

Ada, Oklahoma 109, 110
Albuquerque, Texas 41
Alder Gulch, Montana 76
Allen, A. J. 47
Allen, Buck 12
Allensworth, Billy 99
Anderson, Ham 44
Andrus, Will 105, 107
Angus, W. E. "Red" (Sheriff) 113-115
Antrim, Catherine (McCarty) 53, 54
Antrim, Henry (See Billy the Kid)
Antrim, Joseph 53
Antrim, William Henry Harrison 53
Apocada, Miguel 89
Armentrout, James 120
Arnold, Mace "Winchester Smith" 46, 47
Aten, Ira 104, 106, 107
Austin, Texas 4, 29, 47
Axtell, S. B. (Governor) 54, 64
Aztec Land and Cattle Company 84

B

Baca, Jose Chavez y 64
Baker, Frank 56, 59
Balazan, Mario 6
Bannack, Montana 77
Barber, Amos (Governor) 114
Barrickman, Alec 42, 44
"Battle for the Gray County Seat" 97-100
Beard, John 22, 23
Bearfield, Jim 103
Beaver Smith's Saloon 69
Beckwith, Hugh 8, 9
Beckwith, John 63
Beckwith, Robert 8, 63, 67
Behan, John (Sheriff) 9, 92, 93
Bell, C. S. (Captain) 27-31, 36
Bell County, Texas 49-51
Bell, J.W. (Deputy) 70, 71
Belton 49
Ben Hur 68
Beni, Jules 75, 76
Bennett, Joe 46
Berry, Alpheus W. 119-121, 123
Berry, Beach D. 119-121
Berry, Burchard B. 119, 121-123

Berry, Daniel P. 119, 120, 123
Berry, George 95
Berry, Harriett M. "Hattie" 119, 122
Berry, Viola 120
Berry, William Roy 119-123
Billier, Frederick O. de 111
Billy the Kid 1, 53-73, 98
Bird City, Kansas 121
Black River 64
Blakely, Jake 102, 106
Blanco 23
Blazer, Joseph "Doc" (Dr.) 60, 61
Blazer's Mill 60, 61
Blevins, Andy (See Andy Cooper)
Blevins, Charles 84, 86, 88
Blevins, Hampton 84, 85
Blevins, John 84, 86
Blevins, Mart 84, 85
Blevins, Sam Houston 84, 87
Bliss, Jack 99
Bobbitt, Gus 110
Bolds, George 98, 99
Bonney, William H. (See Billy the Kid)
Border, Peter 22
Bowdre, Charlie 58-62, 64, 65, 67, 69
Bowen, Bill 4, 5, 9, 10
Bowers, George 68
Boyer, Joseph 85, 89
Brady, William (Sheriff) 7, 57-60, 62, 64
Brassell, George 47
Brassell, Philip (Dr.) 47
Brazos River 79
Brent, James 72
Brewer, Richard M. "Dick" 57, 58, 60-62
Bristol, Warren H. (Judge) 70
Britton, F. L. (State Police Chief) 4
Brooks, Ed 99
Brosius, Doc 44
Brown, Arapahoe 113, 114
Brown County, Texas 44
Brown, Henry Newton 59, 60, 62, 64, 66, 67
Brown, Neil 98
Brown, Reuben (Marshal) 44, 46
Bryant, Jeff 105
Buffalo, Wyoming 112-114
"Bulletproof Killer and the Pecos Grudge" 109-110
Burnet County, Texas 22
Busch, Fred (Sheriff) 46

C

Caddo Gap, Arkansas 3
Cahill, Frank 54
Caldwell, William 103
Camp Grant 54
Campbell and Hatch's Billiard Parlor
  (Tombstone) 95
Campbell, Billy 68
Candelaria, José 6
Candelaria, Pilar 7
Canton, Frank M. 112, 113, 115
Capron, Lemuel 121
Carrington, Bob 85
Casey, Robert 9
Casper, Wyoming 112
Castello, Felix 12
Catron, Thomas B. (U.S. District Attorney) 58
Champion, Nathan D. "Nate" 112, 113, 115
Chapman, Houston 68
Chaves, Florencio 67
Chaves, Jose Chaves y 67
Chaves, Martin 64-66
Cherokee County, Texas 82
Cherry Creek 83
Cheyenne County, Kansas 117-119, 121, 122
Cheyenne, Wyoming 112
Chisholm, Dick 34
Chisum, John Simpson 56, 58, 59
Choate, Crockett 28, 32, 33
Choate, John 28-30, 32, 33
Christian, Hiram (Judge) 49-51
Cimarron, Kansas 97-100
Civil War 2, 19, 49, 79
Claiborne, Billy 93
Clanton, Billy 91, 93, 94
Clanton, Ike 92, 93, 95
Clark, Calvin (Dr.) 49-51
Clark, John (Sheriff) 22, 23
Clements, Emmanuel "Manning" 38, 39
Clements, Gibson 38
Clements, Jim 38
Clements, Joe 38
Clinton, Texas 34, 38, 39, 41, 46, 48
Clover, Sam 113
Coates, Fred 112
Cochise County, Arizona 92
Coe, Frank 60, 61, 63, 67
Coe, George 60, 61, 64, 66, 67
Coke, Richard (Governor) 44
Coleman, Texas 47
Comanche, Texas 42, 43, 44, 47
Confederate States of America
  19, 20, 25, 49, 50
Cook, Joe 69
Cooley, Scott 20-23
Cooper, Andy 84, 86
Copeland, John (Sheriff) 64
Corpus Christi, Texas 30
Cox, Bill 47
Cox, Jim 34, 39, 40, 47
Crain, Bill (District Attorney) 45
Crawford, Charlie 65
Crazy Woman Creek 113
Cresman, Jake 40
Crumpton, Zachariah 6, 7, 9
Cruz, Florentino 95
Cuero, Texas 36, 38, 39, 42, 44, 46
Cunningham, V. E. (Captain) 121

D

Daggs, P. P. 85
Daniels, Ben 98
Daniels, T. M. 4
Davis, Edmund J. (Governor) 4, 33, 34, 36, 46
Davis, George 62
Day, Alfred Hays 37, 40
Day, Betty 35
Day, John 35, 36
Day, Robert 35
Day, Will 35, 36, 120
Decatur County, Kansas 118
Denver, Colorado 112
Dewey, A. P. 117, 118
Dewey, C. P. 117-119, 122
Dewey, Chauncey 117-123
"Dewey-Berry Feud, The" 117-123
DeWitt County, Texas 27-29, 35, 36, 41,
  42, 44, 45, 47
Dixon, Bud 44
Dixon, John 13
Dixon, Tom 44
Dodge City, Kansas 97, 98
Dolan, James Joseph 7, 8, 54, 55-59, 62,
  64, 65, 68
Doña Ana County 54
Dowlearn, Bud 40
Drew's Station 91
Dudley, Nathan A. (Colonel, General) 65, 68
Dye, Frederick 120

E

Early, John 49-51
"Earp-Clanton Vendetta, The" 91-96
Earp, James 92, 95
Earp, Morgan 91-96
Earp, Virgil 91-95
Earp, Warren 95

Earp, Wyatt 1, 91, 93, 95
El Paso, Texas 9
Elliott, Joe 112
Ellis, Ben 65
English, J. W. 99
Ensign, Kansas 97
Escambia County, Alabama 45
Evans, Drew 99
Evans, Jessie 54, 56, 62, 65, 67
Evans, Will 99

F

Fairhurst, Ed 99
Ferris, Keane 105
Ferris, Yandell 105
"Feuds of the Horrell Clan" 3-17
Fisher, A. S. 5
Flagg, Jack 113
Flagstaff, Arizona 87
Flemming, Tom 31
Flournoy, Rice S. 48
Foote, Kansas 97
Fort Bend County, Texas 101-105
Fort Davis, Texas 9
Fort Mason, Texas 19, 27
Fort McKinney, Wyoming 114
Fort Russell, Wyoming 115
Fort Stanton, New Mexico 59, 61, 63-67, 81
Fort Sumner, New Mexico 68, 72
Fountain, Albert J. 54
Francis, John W. (Deputy Sheriff) 87
Frazer, G. A. "Bud" 109, 110
Fredericksburg, Texas 22
French, Horace 39
French, Jim (Big Jim) 59, 60, 64, 67
Frost, H. H. 102, 103, 105, 106

G

Galveston News 27
Galveston, Texas 27, 29, 44, 45, 47
García, Apolonia 7
Garrett, Buck 112
Garrett, Pat 1, 69, 72
Garvey, Jim (Sheriff) 102, 105, 106
Georgetown, Texas 4, 5
Gibson, Guilf 105
Gibson, Ned 104
Gibson, Volney 101, 103-105, 107
Giddings, Marsh (Governor) 7
Gilbertson, Ross 112
Gillespie, Bob 85
Gladden, George 22
Globe, Arizona 89

Goliad County, Texas 29
Gonzales County, Texas 38, 39, 44
Gonzales Enquirer 41
Gonzales, Ignacio 60, 67
Gonzales, Juan 8
Graham, Billy 86
Graham, Carson 13
Graham, John 86, 88
Graham, Thomas 88, 89
Graham-Tewksbury Feud 1, 2, 83
Grant, Joe (Texas Red) 68
Graves, Mitch 81
Gray County, Kansas 97-100
Green, Tom 63
Griffin, David 51
Grizell, James 4
Guadalupe River 31
Gutierrez, Celsa 72
Gylam, Jacob L. (Sheriff) 5, 6

H

Hallettsville, Texas 36
Hardin, Jane Bowen 39
Hardin, Joe 42, 44
Hardin, John Wesley 1, 38-44, 47, 67
Harrison, Benjamin (President) 114
Hart, Edward "Little" 8, 9
Hash Knife outfit 84, 85
Haskins, Joe 8
Hasley, Drew 50
Hasley, Sam 49-51
Hayes, Rutherford B. (President) 67
Helena, Texas 28, 31, 40
Helm, Jack 27-31, 33, 34, 36, 39, 41
Hendrix, J. G. 46, 47
Hess, Kansas 97
Hesse, Fred 111
Higgins, John Pinckney "Pink" 10-15
Hill, Tom 56
Hindman, George 60
Hoerster, Dan 22
Hole-in-the-Wall 112
Holliday, John Henry "Doc" 1, 91-95
Holstein, Sim 36, 37
Home Guard 49, 50
Hondo River 63
Hondo Valley 58
Honeycutt, Robert 9
Hood County, Texas 79, 82
"Hoodoo War, The" 1, 17, 19-23
Horrell, Artemisa 4, 5
Horrell, Benjamin 3, 4, 6
Horrell, Elizabeth 3

Horrell, James Martin "Mart" 3-17
Horrell, John 3, 4
Horrell, Samuel, Jr. 3-17
Horrell, Mattie Ann 11
Horrell, Merritt 3-17
Horrell, Samuel 3
Horrell, Sarah 3
Horrell, Thomas 3-17
Horrell War, The 3-17
Horrell, William 3
Horrell-Higgins Feud 3
Houck, James D. (Deputy Sheriff) 85, 87, 88
"House", The 54-59
Houston Light Guard 107
Houston Telegraph 41
Hubbard, Early 3
Hudson, Dick (Deputy Sheriff) 46
Hueco Tanks 9
Huff, Daniel 65
Hunter, Kit 46
Huntsville, Alabama 47

I

Indianola, Texas 42, 45, 47
Ingalls, Kansas 97, 98, 99, 100
Irvine, William 111

J

"Jack Slade and The Julesburg Vendetta" 75-77
Jack Wright's Saloon 44
Jackson County, Texas 47
Jacobs, William 83, 85, 86
Jaybirds 101, 103-105
"Jaybird-Woodpecker Feud, The" 1, 101-107
Jenkins, Jim 4
"Johnson County Invasion, The" 1, 111-115
Johnson County, Wyoming 111, 112, 114, 115
Johnson, "Turkey Creek" Jack 95
Johnson, W. H. 65
Jones, Ben 113
Jones, John B. (Major) 13-15, 17, 22, 23
Jordan, Peter 22
Julesburg, Colorado 75

K

Karnes County, Texas 28, 40
KC Ranch 112, 113
Kelly, Delilah 36
Kelly, Eugene 36, 48
Kelly, Henry 35, 36
Kelly, Wiley 36
Kelly, William 35, 36
Kennan, Tom 8
Kerrville, Texas 36
King, C. W. 8, 9
King, Martin 46, 47
King, Tom 46
Kinney, John W. 54, 58, 65, 67
Kraus, Joe 110

L

L. G. Murphy & Company 54
La Mesilla, New Mexico 54, 70
Lampasas County, Texas 3, 4, 9, 10, 13
Lampasas, Texas 3, 12-15
Lantier, Ike 11
Las Cruces, New Mexico 3
Las Vegas, New Mexico 91
Lauffer, Jake 89
Lavaca County, Texas 36, 37
LeBow, Tom 120
Lee, Robert E. (General) 19, 25
Lincoln County, New Mexico 3, 5, 53-73, 82
Lincoln County War 1, 7, 53, 54, 81, 84
"Lincoln County War and Billy the Kid" 53-73
Lincoln, New Mexico 6, 8, 53-73
Lindley, Jasper 51
Lindley, Jonathan 51
Lindley, Newton 51
Littleton, John (Captain) 35
Live Oak County, Texas 33
Llano River 19, 22
Logan, Harvey 98
Long, John (Jack) 60, 63, 64, 66
Loyal Valley 22
Lucas, A. T. "Bert" 121

M

MacNab, Frank 59, 60, 62-64
Marshall, Texas 38
Martín, Juan (Constable) 6
Martinez, Atanacio (Constable) 57
Mason County, Texas 19, 20, 21, 23
Mason County War, The 1, 19-23
Mason, H. S. 107
Mason, John (Adjutant General, Major) 6
Mason, Texas 19, 21, 22
Masterson, Jim 1, 97-99
Masterson, William Barclay "Bat" 98, 100
Matagorda Bay, Texas 45
Mather, "Mysterious" Dave 91
Mathews, Jacob "Billy" 60, 62-64, 68

Maxwell, Pete 72
McBee, Bob 13
McBride, William J. 119-122
McCarty, Catherine (See Catherine Antrim)
McCarty, Henry (See Billy the Kid)
McCloskey, William H. 59
McCullough, Robert (Sheriff) 121
McFarlane, Earle 106
McFarlane House 106
McKinney, Thomas 72
McLaury, Frank 91-94
McLaury, Tom 91-94
McMasters, Sherman 95
McMullen County, Texas 33
McNelly, Leander H. (Captain) 45, 47
McRae, Jim 50, 51
McSween, Alexander Anderson 56, 57, 60, 62, 64-67
McSween, Susan Ellen 56, 66, 68
Meadows, John 36, 39
Mehan, Andy 93
Melville, Andrew 4
Menardville, Texas 21
Mescalero Apache Indian Reservation 60
Mesilla Valley Independent 54
Middleton, John 58-62, 64-67
Miller, James B. "Deacon Jim" 1, 109-110
Mills, Alexander H. "Ham" (Sheriff) 6, 8
Missouri Plaza 8
Mitchell, A. T. 12
Mitchell, Bill 80-82
Mitchell, Frank 13
Mitchell, Jeff 81
Mitchell, Mack 13
Mitchell, Mary Beckett 81, 82
Mitchell, Maud Jane 81
Mitchell, Nancy 79
Mitchell, Nelson "Cooney" 79, 81
Mitchell, Robert 11-15
"Mitchell-Truitt Affair, The" 79-82
Mitchell-Truitt Feud 1
Mitchell, William Nelson 79
Mitchell's Bend 79
Mogollon Rim 84, 85
Montaño, José 7, 64, 65
Montezuma, Kansas 97
Morgan, J. B. 38
Morris, Harvey 67
Morris, W. B. 33
Morton, Buck 56, 59
Mulvenon, William (Sheriff) 86-89
Murphy, Lawrence Gustave 6-8, 54-56, 59

N

Nacogdoches, Texas 82
Nation, Carry 102
New Orleans, Louisiana 42, 44
Newton, George 87, 89
Northern Wyoming Farmers' and Stock Growers' Association 112
Norton County, Kansas 122

O

O.K. Corral 93, 94, 96
Oak Ranch 118-122
Oakville, Texas 33
O'Folliard, Thomas 67, 68, 70
Olinger, Robert 70, 71
O'Neill, Thomas 120
Osborne Militia 121, 122
Overland Stage Company 75, 76
Overstreet, Rufus 13
Owens, Commodore Perry (Sheriff) 1, 81, 85-87
Owens, Jake 67
Owens, W. J. 81

P

Padilla, Isidro 6
Page, Charley 46
Paine, John 84, 85
Parker, James Wesson (Judge) 102, 105-107
Parnell, Charles 105
Patrón, Isidro 6
Patrón, Juan 6-8
Patterson, Ad 39
Payson, Arizona 87
Peareson, DeRugely 105
Peareson, Dolph 106
Peareson, Sid 106
Pecos County, Texas 109
Pecos, Texas 110
Pecos War 58
Pennington, Texas *28*
Pensacola, Florida 47
Peppin, George 60, 63-67
Perry, R. C. "Rufe" (Captain) 21
Picacho, New Mexico 8
Pickens, Abraham 42, 45
Pickett, Tom 69, 84
Pierce, A. H. "Shanghai" 27
Pleasant Valley 2, 83-86
"Pleasant Valley War, The" 83-89
Pleasants, Henry Clay (Judge) 42

Plummer, Henry 77
Poe, John W. 72
Pollard, Alabama 44
Posse Comitatus Act 65
Powder River 112
Powell, Buck 64
Prescott, Arizona 87-89
Prices Creek 36
Pridgen, Bolivar (State Senator) 36, 42, 43, 45, 48
Pridgen, Wiley 42

R

Ragland, H. 40
Randlett, James (Captain) 9
Ravenswood Ranch Cover, 75
Rawlins County, Kansas 118, 119
Ray, Nick 113, 115
Reconstruction Acts 25
Reed's Lake 49
Reeves County, Texas 109
Regulators (New Mexico) 58-64, 66, 67, 69
Regulators (Texas) 27, 28, 33-35
Reicheldeffer, Charlie 98, 99
"Reprisal in Bell County" 49-51
Reynolds, J. H. (Sheriff) 98, 100
Reynolds, J. J. (Governor) 33
Richmond, Texas 101, 104, 107
Riley, A. T. 98
Riley County 118
Riley, John Henry 55-58, 62
Rinconada, The 60
Ringgold, John 22
Rio Hondo River 8
Rio Penasco 59
Rivers, Frank (a.k.a. John Long) 62
Roberts, Andrew L. "Buckshot" 60-62
Roberts, Jim 85, 89
Roberts, Mose 86
Robertson, E. B. (Deputy Sheriff) 121
Romero, Vicente 67
Rose, Al 88, 89
Roswell, New Mexico 8
Rudabaugh, Dave 69
Ruidoso River 5
Ruidoso Valley 56, 58
Runnel, John 44
Rynerson, William L. (District Attorney) 58, 68

S

Salazar, Jose 68
Salazar, Yginio 67, 71

Salina, Kansas 120
San Agustin Pass 3
San Andres Mountains 3
San Antonio River 31, 40
San Antonio, Texas 51
San Patricio 33, 64, 68
San Patricio County 27-31
Sanchez, Jose Maria 67
Santa Fe, New Mexico 53
Saunders, Ab 63, 64
Schmidt, Frank 107
Scott, Jerry 4, 5, 7, 9, 11
Scroggins, John 60
Scurlock, Josiah "Doc" 58, 63-68
Seguro, Miguel (Manuel Segovia) 62
Selman, John 67
Selman, Tom 67
Selman's Scouts 67
Seven Rivers 9, 58, 62, 63, 65
Shamblin, J. H. 103
Shaw, James 81
Sherman County, Kansas 118
Shield, Elizabeth 66
Short, G. W. 4
Short, Mark 4
Sigsby, Bob 85
Silver City, New Mexico 53
Singer, Fred 98, 99
Skidmore, F. O. 28, 31
Slade, Joseph Alfred "Jack" Cover, 75-77
Slade, Virginia Cover, 75, 77
Slater, Benjamin F. 120
Slaughter, Gabriel 43, 47
Smith, Robbie 106
Smith, Sam 59, 64, 66, 67
Smith, Tom 112
Smith, Van C. 8, 9
Smolly, Jim 38
Soule, Asa T. 97, 98
Spence, Pete 95
Spencer, Ran 27
Spradley, A. J. (Sheriff) 82
Spur, Texas 16
St. Francis, Kansas 121
St. Johns, Arizona 87
Standard, Jess 12
Stanley, Steve 8
Stephens, Steve 60
Stilwell, Frank 95
Stinking Springs 69
Sun, Charlie 54
Sutton, Laura 39, 42, 43
"Sutton-Taylor Feud, The" 25-48
Sutton, William 34-39, 42, 43, 46, 47
Swain, J. H. 44

T

TA Ranch 111, 113-115
Taylor, Amanda 35, 36
Taylor, Bill 43-45, 47, 48
Taylor, Charley 34, 35
Taylor, Creed 25, 26, 28-31
Taylor, Hays 25-28, 35
Taylor, Jim 35-38, 40-44, 46, 47
Taylor, John 48
Taylor, Martin 33
Taylor, Phillip "Doboy" 25-*28*, 35, 36
Taylor, Pitkin 35, 37, 42
Taylor, Scrap 39, 40, 44
Taylor, William Riley, Sr. 27, 42
Taylor, Susan 35, 36
Taylor, William Riley, Jr. "Buck" 27, 34, 43
Tennelle, George 38, 39, 44
Terrell, Zeke 11
Terry, Ben 13
Terry, Kyle 103, 104
Teschemacher, Hubert 111
Tewksbury, Ed 85, 86, 89
Tewksbury, Jim 85, 86, 89
Tewksbury, John 83, 86
Texanna, Texas 47
Texas Rangers 20, 21, 44, 45, 47, 104, 109, 110
Texas Rangers' Frontier Battalion 13, 17, 22, 34
Texas State Police 34, 36, 38, 45
The Santa Fe Ring 58
Thomas County, Kansas 118
Thomaston, Texas 43
Tilghman, Bill 1, 97-99
Timpson, Texas 81
Tombstone, Arizona 9, 91, 92, 94, 95
Tonto Basin, Arizona 83, 84, 86
Topeka, Kansas 121
Truitt, Ike 81
Truitt, Jim 81, 82
Truitt, Julia 81, 82
Truitt, Sam 81
Trujillo, Seferino 6
Tucker, Edward 120
Tucker, G. R. 112
Tucker, Tom 84, 85
Tucson, Arizona 95
Tuggle, Kute 44
Tumlinson, Joe (Captain) 29, 30, 33, 34, 39-42, 45
Tunstall, John Henry 56-58, 60-64, 68
Turner, Ben 8
Turner, Marion 63, 64

U

Underwood, Joe 88
Union Army (See United States Army)
Union Pacific Railroad 112
United States Army 19, 25, 67

V

Vanhorn, J. J. (Colonel) 114
Vaughan, J. F. 16
Victoria Advocate 29
Vigilance Committee 77
Virginia City, Montana 76, 77
Virginia Dale 76

W

Waco, Texas 16, 38
Wade, W. T. 105, 107
Wagner, George 89
Waite, Fred 57, 58, 60, 62, 67
Waldrup, Jim "Buck" 13
Walker, Bill 113
Wallace, Lew (Governor) 68
Walz, Edgar 68
Warner, David C. 6
Warnick, Bill 8
Watson, Newt F. 98, 99
Webb, Charles (Deputy Sheriff) 44, 47
Webb, John 69
Westfall, Henry *28*
White, Doc 36, 39
White, Jim 44
Whitecraft, Allen 4
Wier, Billy 64
Wilburn, Aaron O. 8, 9
Wild Bunch, The 98
Williams, Thomas G. (Captain) 4, 10
Williamson, Tim 20, 22
Wilson, Billy 69
Wilson, Charles 120
Wilson, Clyde 120-122
Wilson, James 9
Wilson, John 60
Wilson, Squire 68
Winship, Albert 120
Wolcott, Frank (Major) 111, 113-115
Woodpeckers 101, 103, 105, 106
Woods, Powell 12
Worley, John (Deputy Sheriff) 20, 21
Wortley Hotel 70, 71
Wren, William R. 11, 13-16
Wyoming Stock Growers Association 111-113

Y

Yavapai County 86
Yeager, Red 77
Yorktown 28, 30, 31

Z

Zamora, Francisco 67
Zulick, C. Meyer (Governor) 87

www.ingramcontent.com/pod-product-compliance
Lightning Source LLC
Chambersburg PA
CBHW071501080526
44587CB00014B/2172